Bringing Respect Back

Communicating Without The Conflict

Copyright © 2013 by Don Olund

Cover design by Renee Barratt - www.thecovercounts.com

Illustrations by Marcy Braasch

Diagrams by Don Olund

All rights reserved.
No part of this book may be reproduced in any form or by any electronic or mechanical means including information storage and retrieval systems, without permission in writing from the author. The only exception is by a reviewer, who may quote short excerpts in a review.
Printed in the United States of America

First Printing: October 2013

ISBN 978-1494286316

Don Olund

Bringing Respect Back

Communicating Without The Conflict

*To my beautiful Marian. You are God's gift to me.
I continue to marvel at your simplicity and complexity. Indeed, you are my
rose.*

Acknowledgements

A PROJECT OF this nature was not created in a vacuum but emerged from a collection of people who fed into my life, teaching and modeling respect. I have also been blessed to have several others who could see my potential and inspired me to find my passion and pursue my purpose. Finally, I owe a debt of gratitude to the individuals who helped on this writing project to make my first book something I am very proud to share with the public.

I begin with a deep and profound sense of gratitude to my family. My parents taught us from an early age the value of respect. It was easy to catch just by observing how they lived and conducted themselves at home and in social settings. We were a close family, due in large part to the youngest in our family, my brother Tom. Born with a mental disability, his needs required a united effort to care for him. It turns out Tom helped us more than we helped him. His winsome personality, innocence, and genuine affection for every person he met, taught us how to respect people from all walk of life. We remain a very close family to this day.

Being a father has taught me many lessons about respect. One of the things I learned from my dad was the importance of being present but also allowing your kids room to grow and figure things out for themselves. Easier said than done. However, following my dad's advice has proven to be true. I have watched my children, Candace, Justin, and Jordan experience the bumps and bruises of growing up, including periods that were very turbulent. Today I am proud to see how each on is finding their way in life and emerging into their adult years successfully.

I would like to thank the professors who also made a huge impact in my academic and professional life. Unbeknownst to me, a few years later they would later invite me back to the university to serve on the faculty. Dr. Kate Sori and Dr. Shannon Dermer supervised my program and invited me to join them as a contributing author in clinical literature. Thank you Kate and Shannon for pouring into my life and inspiring me to write. Your tag-teaming efforts finally got through to me and I took the plunge. Thank you for believing in me.

I would also like to express gratitude to Dr. Shea Dunham who inspired to keep writing even during tough times. She supported me when I was going through a painful loss and the project turned out to be my best contribution at that time. Thank you Dr. Jon Carlson for blazing the trail for many of us who have benefited from your vision to create a counseling program that is producing not only professional counselors, but authors and world changers.

I want to thank my mentors, Dr. Steve Warner and Dr. Charlie Alcorn. Steve, you were my pastor, colleague, confident, and now a very close friend. You taught me how to wear a suit (private joke), walk through the valley, and to live a congruent life in my Christian faith. Rarely, a day goes by that I don't think about something you said publicly or privately that has shaped my life. We have walked with each other through tough times. I know you are a speed dial away if I need you. I know you feel the same way.

Charlie, as my counselor, you came into my life over twenty years ago when I was an emotional wreck. You know me better than anyone. Along my journey we have broken the code of ethics regarding dual relationship. You remain my counselor, but we have become colleagues too. More than that, you are both a father to me and a friend. It was your words that gave me the blessing to become a counselor. Thank you for pouring into my life.

I would like to thank those who worked specifically on this book, for their contributions. Thank you Nick Andrus for your tireless work in helping me see the broader vision for this project and your creative ideas that are now being put into action. Devin Bustin, thank you for doing the editing work and helping me to write in ways to keep the reader interested. Finally, I want to thank Renee Barratt and Marcy Braasch for their amazing artistic contribution. Renee you captured the essence of the book in visual form. Marcy, you did a great job illustrating the absurdity of disrespect and offering a visual representation of how things look differently when respect comes into the picture.

I reserve my final acknowledgment to the person who has made the deepest impact in my life. This place belongs to my wife Marian. Some might say our paths crossed serendipitously, we would say spiritually. We met in a church at a time when neither of us were not looking for a relationship. There is an obvious sense of mutual respect in our marriage and it informs my writing on the subject. Marian was the first person who encouraged me to write. It took several attempts to get through my thick skull, but apparently she saw something at the time I did not see.

Marian, I owe you a debt of gratitude for your contribution, not simply to this book, but more importantly, to my life. Your steadfast support and faith in me as a writer and communicator has kept me going at times when I wanted to quit. It's not just your words that inspire me. Rather, it is how you profoundly model respect in your personal and professional life. This is one among the many things I admire about you.

With much love and respect,

Don

Preface

In 2006 Justin Timberlake rocked the musical world with his hit "Sexy Back". In an interview Timberlake stated that the first line that came to him was "bringing sexy back". Of course the song struck a chord (no pun intended) with the audience and rose to the top of the Billboard charts for several weeks and Timberlake won multiple awards.

Honestly, I thought the title of the song was weird especially in our sex-crazed culture. Call me out-of-touch but I'm not sure sexy needed a "come back". If anything maybe it could be dialed down a bit. Don't get me wrong, I enjoy sex as much as the average person. However, does everything in life revolve around sex or being sexy? I don't think so. We are more than one dimensional right?

The song led me to ponder a question, *"What do we need to bring back?"* It didn't take me too long to figure out the answer, at least from my perspective. What's missing in our culture is not sexy, it's respect. We have sexy coming at us from every direction, but respect is often hard to find. What we see more today is disrespect. It has seeped into every social institution in our country: family, school, work, government, and religion.

As a licensed clinical counselor, certified executive coach and communication specialist, I help clients break negative relationship patterns. When I ask couples or families to summarize their problem in one word or phrase, *"lack of respect"* is by far the number one response. A common lament is, *"I don't feel respected by my* (fill in the blank)." The absence of respect comes out in the way people communicate and how they treat one another. I call it a dance of disrespect.

The dance of disrespect is not pretty. It tends to bring out the ugly in people. I visualize a postmodern version of the "Monster Mash" made popular by Bobby "Boris" Pickett & the Crypt Kickers in the early sixties. Except in this dance nobody is having fun! Every morning the ritual begins as members of a family don their monster attire and ready themselves for the mash pit. Have you ever wondered how family members can act like monsters toward each other but be kind around others? Strange phenomenon.

So after countless hours of counseling and hearing the cries of clients complaining about disrespect, I decided it is high time we bring back a classic dance. I call it a dance of respect. In contrast to disrespect, this is a beautiful dance that brings out the best in people. Based on basic interpersonal concepts like reciprocity, accommodation, and welfare, mutual respect emphasizes communicating to hear and be heard, understand and be understood, care and be cared for by others.

The book follows a family of four, Kevin and Heidi Hughes, and their two teenage kids: Brandon age seventeen, and Stacy who is fifteen years old. In the first chapter, you get a peek into a typical morning in their home where the dance of disrespect is performed flawlessly. I use this family to illustrate the elements of disrespect and the effect it has on the poor quality of their relationships including the tone it establishes in the home.

In succeeding chapters, I walk you through the process of what it looks like to bring respect back into a family. You will see for example, how the adults come to terms with themselves, their lack of self-respect and how it plays out in the marriage. As the couple begin to bring respect back into their marriage we will see the effect it starts to have on their teenagers. In succeeding chapters we observe how they bring respect back in the family, including the sibling relationships.

As you will read in the first chapter there was a time a few generations ago when respect was the dance du jour. Citizens banded together to fight through the Great Depression, sandwiched between two world wars. Families were tight-knit, held together by marriages that were strong and a parenting structure that provided safety and freedom within limits. Kids knew right from wrong and for the most part, followed the rules because they knew consequences would be enforced by parents who ruled the roost.

Back in the day, some authority figures, fathers in particular, took a harsh, punitive approach. The pendulum of authority swung too far. Respect was shown out of fear, not love. Over time this parenting style began to have a toxic effect in the family. Beginning in the sixties, a new generation began to react to authoritarianism. However, the overcorrection resulted in a drastic pendulum swing to the opposite end where leadership became more passive and young adults focused more on individual freedom and entitlement. In succeeding generations, personal responsibility gave way to personal rights, interdependence to independence, we to me. The net result is a lowering bar of respect.

In chapter two I illustrate the steps in both dances. I will show how the dance of disrespect establishes adversarial interactions, always ending in distance. In the dance of respect, I highlight the movements that shift the relationship from adversarial to an alliance between people who show genuine care for one another.

Chapter three is key because to bring respect back it has to begin with ourselves. I devote an entire chapter to bringing self-respect back in your life. Most of us tend to think we have self-respect, yet when I break down the elements, I am sure you will find, like I have, there are some areas to work on.

Next, in chapter four, I move from self-respect to bringing respect back into your marriage/relationship. Here, I look at marital drift, what causes it, and how if left unaddressed, sets the couple up for the dance of disrespect. As in all the chapters, I highlight specifically how couples can bring respect back into their relationship.

In chapters five and six, I write extensively about family relationships, using the Hughes family to address disrespect in sibling interactions. I also introduce the concept of "influential parenting" an approach that balances the extremes of punitive and passive parenting.

My writing shifts from the family to social settings in succeeding chapters. In chapter seven, I examine the workplace to see how the absence of respect has affected the employment sector. Here is where adults spend the majority of their day working. To gain insight on the subject I interview a few business owners and managers to get their views.

Chapter eight centers on bringing respect back in our society. Moving from the microcosm to the macrocosm, I explore a few of the barriers that inhibit people from showing respect to those who are different. Here, I offer some perspective and directives for you to consider. It is one of my favorite chapters.

I devoted chapter nine to help people who are in relationships with others who seemingly do not know how, or choose not to show respect. These are the most difficult relationships to navigate, especially if the person plays an important role in your life. You will see how Heidi struggles as an adult in her relationship with her demanding mother to establish healthy boundaries. I will address how to handle one-sided relationships.

Finally, in chapter ten I talk about the benefits of bringing respect back in your life. I summarize the key points in the book and tie them into positive outcomes you will likely experience in your personal life and interpersonal relationships. The benefits are truly worth the effort of bringing respect back. As you read and apply these strategies I think you will agree.

As you read this book, I ask that you do some introspection. It is easy to read a book like this and think about all the people in your life who need to read it so they can finally show you some respect. How about you? Do you respect yourself? Are you sure? Do you respect others? While writing this book I confess that it makes me think about areas in which I lack respect for myself and could do better showing respect to others.

I encourage you to take inventory of yourself as you read. Jot down some notes. Try using some of the dance steps I teach. They do work. It takes practice and commitment to the dance, but it will make a difference in your life and relationships. So remember now, the focus is on you learning the dance. Got it? Okay, let's move to the dance floor and get ready to learn.

Contents

Chapter 1: What Happened to Respect?	**19**
What Happened to Good Old Fashioned Respect?	20
Erosion of Respect	22
Purpose for Writing	24
Chapter 2: The Dance of Respect	**27**
The 3-Step Dance of Disrespect	29
The 6-Step Dance of Respect	31
Chapter 3: Bringing Self-Respect Back	**39**
Self-Acceptance: I'm Okay with Me	41
Self-Care: I Matter	44
Self-Responsibility: I can manage my life	48
Where You Are and Where to Go from Here	52
Chapter 4: Bringing Respect Back Into Your Marriage	**57**
Marital Drift	58
Bringing Respect Back in Civility	62
Bringing Respect Back in Friendship	72
Bringing Respect Back in Intimacy	74
Where to Start Bringing Respect Back	80
Chapter 5: Bringing Respect Back Into The Family	**83**
Families Upside Down	84
First Move: Parents Model Respect with Each Other	87
Second Move: Parents Show Respect to Their Kids	89
Third Move: Parents Set the Respect Bar For the Family	91
The Dance of Respect in Action	97
Where Do You Need to Start?	100

Chapter 6: Influential Parenting:
How to Get Your Kids to Step Up — 104
Principle #1: Influential Parents Instill a
Sense of Value in their Children. — 106
Principle #2: Influential Parents Are
the Primary Providers of Their Kids' Needs — 108
Principle #3: Influential Parents,
Give their Kids a Sense of Purpose. — 110
Principle #4: Influential Parents
Establish Structure in Their Family — 113
Principle #5: Influential Parents Provide
Moral and Spiritual Guidance for Their Kids — 115
Principle # 6: Influential Parents Respect Personal Power — 119
Principle #7: Influential Parents Instill Social Values — 122
Three Key Things to Remember About Influential Parents — 124

Chapter 7: Bringing Respect Back in the Workplace — 126
Disrespect in the Workplace — 127
Creating a Culture of Respect in the Workplace — 137
What You Can Do to Bring Respect Back in the Workplace — 141

Chapter 8: Bringing Respect Back In Society — 146
Bringing Respect Back Begins at Home — 148
Use a Single Lens of Respect — 151
Develop the Art of Curiosity — 153
Replace Hypocrisy with Some Humility — 154
Show Tolerance While Holding to Your Values — 157
Find Common Ground to Stand On — 159
Bringing Respect Full-Circle — 160

Chapter 9: When Respect Doesn't Happen — 165
Types of One-Sided Relationships — 168
Maintaining Self-Respect in a Disrespectful Relationship — 172
Grieve the Relationship You Envisioned — 174
Adjust Your Expectations for the Relationship — 177
Modify Your Boundaries Accordingly — 178
Fill the Void with Healthy Relationships — 182
Taking Action — 183

Chapter 10: What You Can Expect When Respect Happens — 187

Refined Sense of Self	188
Keener Sense of Purpose & Direction	190
A Healthier Lifestyle — Less Stress and More Energy	191
Greater Understanding of Others	193
Improved Communication and Conflict Resolution Skills	197
Deeper, More Trusting Relationships	199
Where to Start Getting Respect Back	201
Final Remarks	204

Chapter One

What Happened to Respect?

ALL IS QUIET in the Hughes household, but that is about to change. It's six o'clock in the morning and the alarm goes off. No, it's not Sonny and Cher singing, "I Got You Babe," but it does feel like *Groundhog Day*. Kevin Hughes hits the snooze button and resumes his fetal position. Heidi, Kevin's wife, is already rehearsing the day's activities. She rolls her eyes at Kevin whose back is turned toward her and thinks, *He's so useless.*

Heidi dreads the next hour because she knows she's in for another battle. Her strategy is to enter the easiest combat zone and work her way to the hardest. First stop, her fifteen year-old daughter Stacy. No need to wake her up: Stacy gets up before the alarm too because she needs to arm herself for battle when she meets her so-called friends at school.

As Heidi enters her room, Stacy greets her with, "Thanks mom, you've ruined my day." Stacy continues with a tirade about how her mother hates her because she didn't wash her outfit, forgot to buy her hair gel, and won't carpool her friends to the mall after school.

The shouting match between mother and daughter wakes Kevin from his slumber, albeit in contempt. He enters the fray by yelling at his wife for being so hard on their daughter.

With battles one and two in full force, Heidi heads to ground zero, seventeen year-old Brandon's room. Brandon, the nocturnal member of the family, was playing video games into the wee hours of the morning. Heidi's heart races as she begins the morning ritual. She knows what comes next.

"Brandon, it's time to get up for school." She braces for the shot across the bow.

"Get the f&*# out of my room," he shouts. The barrage of verbal attacks and threats goes back and forth between mother and son. Kevin, who surrendered to defeat years ago, walks past the room, leaving his wife alone in the battle. By the time the Hughes family leaves for work and school, nobody is talking. Actually, they cannot wait to get away from each other.

Does the battle end at home? No, it has just begun. Each enters a new war zone where the battle is real and wounds cut deep. They enter a world without respect.

What Happened To Good Old Fashioned Respect?

Something's missing in our culture. It's been absent for quite some time. Those of us in the baby boomer generation can tell things are different. You can see it in the way people interact. It's not the way we were raised, not to say our parents got it right. However, we were taught a very basic manner in our interactions with others. We were taught respect.

Somehow, we have lost our respect for respect. In other words, respect is no longer sacred in relationships. Respect has been replaced by values that reflect self-centeredness, entitlement, and self-gratification. As a culture, we are becoming more self-absorbed: we think more about ourselves than others. Consequently, relationships lack depth, trust, and meaningful connection.

Observe the lack of respect at home. Notice it in the way couples behave. In the early stages of the relationship, couples trip over each other showing respect. Hit the fast forward button and the same couple may have a look of disinterest, perhaps distain in their interactions. What happened? One might say they fell out of love. It is more likely that they lost respect for each other and their love followed suit.

Respect is also missing in parent-child interactions. I'm not just talking about the typical pattern that emerges during adolescence. Take a look at the playground, daycare center, or play dates at McDonalds. Young children are extending the terrible twos into the terrible teens. Kids order parents to do their bidding. If they don't get their own way, then comes the screaming and flopping on the ground until their demands are met. Some kids use words to flay their parents and showcase their power in the family. In many households, the hierarchy has been inverted with the kids holding court and parents serving as subjects.

Speaking of kids, sibling and social relationships are prime examples of the missing link of respect. Sibling rivalry has morphed into sibling terrorism! Back in the day, kids would get along most of the time and bicker on occasion. Parents would not allow too much disruption. The fights we used to get into with our brothers and sisters would look like utopia compared to today.

The majority of kid interactions today exhibits a conflict tone. Siblings battle for their parents' attention, affection, time, toys, and other privileges. Score keeping is a ritual among siblings. Unfairness is met with fights, stealing, blaming, and screaming at each other and parents too. Parents might as well wear referee shirts because they are constantly involved in breaking up fights. Often, the solution is to give each child their own room, complete with media center: TV, computer, video games, cell phone, and so on. Unfortunately, this doesn't work because kids barge into each other's rooms and take what doesn't belong to them.

Brace yourself. It's not any better at school. As children grow into adolescence, particularly in junior high and high school, the lack of respect is glaring. The social network amplifies the problem. Young people use the internet to connect, and sometimes to attack. Texts, tweets, and Facebook are the conduits for verbal assaults obscure from adult observation. Anxious kids, fixated on their network devices, monitor their ranking in social groups, often worrying that they might be unfriended by an entire group because one friend is mad at them. The more extreme forms of cyber bullying contribute to adolescent anxiety, depression, and in some cases, suicide.

Not only is respect missing on the playground, but it is becoming harder to find in the classroom. One major complaint among teachers is the level of disrespect students exhibit toward them. Rudeness is considered acceptable behavior, the norm in adolescent interactions. Students see nothing wrong with talking back to their teachers and will challenge them in front of their peers. This display of power is not only blatant disrespect, but if not handled properly will hinder teachers' ability to maintain control of a classroom. Moreover, the atmosphere of disrespect diminishes the quality of education students receive.

The workplace is another arena that lacks respect and it goes both ways. Employees don't feel respected by their employers and visa-versa. One of the main contributors to a lack of productivity on the job is low morale in the work environment. Disrespect is at the heart of the problem. Disharmony among coworkers is heightened by the negative patterns of interaction that govern their relationships. Concepts like manners, decorum, and politeness seem obsolete in work culture.

The inversion of hierarchy prominent in many families can also be observed at work. In the seventies, there was no confusion about who established and enforced the rules. If you didn't comply with the expectations of management, you were terminated, no questions asked. This style of management has given way to a "don't rock the boat" style that is all about avoiding litigation from disgruntled employees. With the balance of power clearly on the side of the employee, company policy and rules are not respected.

I could go on and talk about the lack of respect in other institutions: church and government. There are also countless examples of disrespect in the entertainment industry, particularly reality TV where rudeness boosts ratings. Families feasting on a heavy diet of this type of entertainment will likely form unhealthy relationships. I think you get the point.

Erosion Of Respect

Our culture did not abandon respect overnight. Rather, it has been a slow, methodical process that likely began at the start of the baby boomer generation. The generation that emerged during World War II knew what it meant to sacrifice for our country. Men went off to war, while the women went off to work. People respected our country, their family, and their neighbors. Those in positions of authority, beginning with the President of the United States, government leaders, police officers, ministers, employers, and teachers were esteemed and shown respect. Life was hard, but people pitched in together to get through the tough times.

However, when the war ended, the mentality of that generation was to make life easier for their children. They did not want them to lack the things they didn't have, so parents worked tirelessly to give their kids the American Dream. With world war in the rearview mirror, men returned to work and women returned home to raise children. Thus the Baby Boomers were birthed, a postwar generation reaping the benefits of the sacrifices made by their parents and grandparents.

If you were born between 1946 and 1964, you were lucky although you likely didn't feel this way. You came along after the first world war, the Great Depression, and WWII. Life was simple, not complicated, and your world was structured so you would not have to experience hardship. Family meals, morning and evening, were a part of the routine of family life. Prosperity was the clarion call that drove your parents to sacrifice so that you would not go without, nor suffer the hardship they endured. Up to that point in history, the boomers were the most prosperous, healthiest, and secure generation in the nation's history.

As our nation entered a period of affluence, boomers were the first of succeeding generations to experience entitlement. A booming industrial force brought a fleet of new automobiles, televisions, home appliances, air conditioning, and many other conveniences that made life less burdensome. Parents taught and enforced rules in the family and kids for the most part had chores to do. Yet, generally, it was an idyllic life for most people in the boomer generation.

During the sixties, respect for authority weakened as world events took shape. Vietnam, an unpopular war, caught the attention of the first line of boomers entering adulthood. For the first time in years, young adults were questioning authority figures from the White House to their parents' house. They spoke out against the inequalities in our system relative to race and gender. In their view, the American Dream was a facade and people were plastic. Voices of disrespect were loud and unfiltered as college students took over campuses, burned American flags, tuned out the capitalistic ideal and tuned in to freedom, peace, and love.

The countercultural and civil rights movement of the sixties created a platform for the boomer generation to voice opposition to institutions and systems that were oppressing people. Abuse of power prevalent in government, business, education, religion, not to mention the family, was intolerable to boomers. Taking a stand was important, but the message was obscured by the methods. Angry youth voiced their opposition in a manner that compounded the fracture rather than solving the problem. Protesters turned to mockery, flag burning, referring to police as pigs, and other antics to voice their disrespect. While the movement brought some positive change, the influence would have been greater if the voices would have taken a more respectful tone.

As the movement attracted more followers, it started degenerating internally. Some in the "turned on" generation were abusing their bodies and dying young. Overnight, Haight Asbury, the Mecca of the peace movement, became an unsafe zone marked by drug overdose, rape, and murder. Some leaders of the movement were selling out as they seized opportunity for personal gain. The children of capitalists did not fall far from the tree. As disenchantment grew, the countercultural movement dwindled to a few communes sprinkled across the American landscape.

In the seventies, the boomers reentered the system, obtaining degrees, landing corporate jobs, and chasing the American Dream. Cocaine succeeded marijuana as the drug du jour. The eighties became known as the decade of greed-fueled consumerism as boomer parents gave birth to Generation X. Over the next thirty years, an Age of Entitlement infused our culture, pitting individuals in the most intimate of relationships against each other in a battle for power. Idealism gave way to indulgence. Image trumped integrity. Me versus you. My needs versus yours. We've come a long way, baby, and the respect for our fellow citizen that united our nation and defined our institutions is missing in action.

Purpose For Writing

I decided to write this book not as a rant, but a resource to bring respect back into our personal lives and interpersonal relationships. In so doing, perhaps we can influence culture to bring respect back as a highly revered social value. In my work as a professional counselor, executive coach, and educator, I see how fragmented relationships are due to the disrespectful way people interact. Spouses feel misunderstood, unappreciated, and unloved. Parents look battle-worn, feel inept and powerless as their children walk all over them. Kids also feel disrespected by their parents who are more worried about appearances than the actual problems they have.

In many cases, families are trying to get along, but they don't know how to communicate properly, manage conflicts, or how to regulate their emotions. Consequently, they develop patterns of interacting that break down, cause emotional distress, and distance. I call this a dance of disrespect. I'll describe this dance in detail in the next chapter, but for now I'll offer a brief introduction.

The dance of disrespect occurs so often that it is performed flawlessly. Of course, I say this not as a compliment, but to emphasize how frequently individuals in a family disrespect one another. Sadly, disrespect is often the norm, but the negative effect it has on relationships is disturbing.

Let's take the effect on energy as an example. In a conflict, an emotional energy drain often exceeds the issue people fight over. A dispute over putting a dirty glass in the dishwasher can go nuclear in a matter of minutes. The residual effect of this conflict may sap energy levels throughout the day if the matter isn't resolved, which is often the case when disrespect permeates a relationship. Repeated patterns of disrespect leave people feeling drained. To cope, they will likely avoid each other just to prevent another argument.

In the next chapter, I will introduce the dance of respect. Like most dances, it involves a sequence of steps people follow that help them connect. Contrary to the dance of disrespect, which drains energy, the dance of respect is energy-enriching. Matters of conflict are resolved quickly and efficiently, preserving closeness and leaving plenty of energy in the emotional tank for enjoyment and intimacy. Respect opens the portals of communication, allowing people to listen, understand, and respond to one another with kindness and support.

I will teach you how to do the dance of respect in marriage, family interactions, and in public arenas such as work. However, before you learn how to dance with others, I want to teach you how to dance solo, the dance of self-respect. If you can do this, you will know how to relate with others respectfully.

Put on your dancing shoes. Get ready to master the dance of respect.

Chapter Two

The Dance of Respect

The Hughes split in different directions. Stacy is chauffeured by mom to high school, an unpleasant task for Heidi because Stacy is a ball of anxiety, obsessing about everything from how she looks to her friendship with Katie she claims is tanking because they like the same guy. Heidi's attempts to calm Stacy down only amp her up. By the time the car arrives at school, Stacy is scowling and Heidi is fighting back the tears, exhausted before she even gets to work where, by the way, she will encounter more of the same.

Brandon doesn't take rides from adults. He'd rather walk to school than be seen with his parents. High school is a waste of time for the most part. He goes to school to see his friends and to keep his parents off his back. Brandon views high school like the military. *Tour of duty. Three years down, one to go, unless I decide to go AWOL.* When you observe Brandon at school, you quickly learn he is not a good soldier. In terms of academic focus, it doesn't exist. His classroom behavior is a teacher's nightmare. He opts for disruption over discussion. When the teacher confronts him, he cuts a joke or makes a rude comment. Brandon is a master of disrespect.

Kevin uses the train ride downtown to get his game face on. Another day, another battle at the office. As a mid-manager in a corporate business, Kevin is sandwiched between two groups of expectations. Upper management wants to see the two Ps, production and profit. The employees beneath him expect the two Es, ease and entitlement. When Kevin doesn't deliver, he hears it and it doesn't sound pleasant.

Does this story sound vaguely familiar? For many it does, because we live in a culture of disrespect. As I discussed in the previous chapter, it is pervasive in every institution: family, work, education, government, and religion. We cannot escape it. Does it mean we have to engage in it? In other words, if someone is being disrespectful to me, do I push back? The short answer is no. What would the outcome be if you reciprocated? Think about the Hughes family. They routinely wound each other with words and actions that drive them apart.

Respect and disrespect: Each dance involves steps partners follow that create the rhythm or pattern. In the dance of disrespect, the steps are *reactive* (quick and impulsive), while in the dance of respect, the steps are *responsive* (slow and measured). In both scenarios, the pattern of interaction between the dancers is reciprocal. For example, when a dance partner acts in a disrespectful manner, their partner will react similarly, which sets the dance in motion. Disrespect moves back and forth. On the contrary, in the dance of respect, one partner initiates a gesture of respect and their partner responds in like manner, creating a pattern of mutual respect.

So, how might the dance of respect have gone between Heidi and Stacy on the drive to school? When Heidi noticed Stacy obsessing about her friend Katie liking the same guy she did, her mom could initiate the dance by validating her daughter's feelings:

"I can tell this situation leaves you with mixed emotions—your angry that she likes a guy you told her you liked, and worried it might end up hurting your friendship."

This response to Stacy's anxiety is calming, because it validates her feelings and conveys an understanding of her concern, in a respectful manner. Stacy might likely reciprocate by sharing more of her concern with her mother. Heidi may respond by sharing a similar event in her life growing up, how it affected her and how it was eventually resolved. This mother and daughter dance would have reduced anxiety and bonded the relationship. Heidi's tears in the parking lot would not be of hurt and disrespect, but of comfort and connection made with her daughter.

In my work as a family counselor, I observe people doing the dance of disrespect on a regular basis. The pattern of interaction causes hurt, distance, and mistrust. Neither party is having much fun, yet they can't seem to get out of this rhythm. In the initial phase of counseling, the pattern emerges as the family members discuss the problem. It is clear they are not enjoying the interaction as emotions rise with each counter move. Still, they continue this dance until one is exhausted or hurt and withdraws.

Once I identify the pattern, I describe the dance step-by-step, highlighting the harmful elements and how the dance ends in distance, not the closeness they desire. Because they have become proficient in the dance, it becomes a first order of response in conflict. The pattern is ingrained in their style of interaction, a self-protective measure, based on fear and mistrust. The goal in counseling is to break the negative pattern by creating a healthy one. Before I outline those vital steps, let's look at the 3-Step dance of disrespect.

The 3-Step Dance Of Disrespect

Step One: Engaging Your Partner

Typically, this begins with a negative attitude toward your partner for a real or perceived wrong. For example, Stacy thought her mother was out to ruin her day because she didn't meet her expectations. When Heidi entered her room, Stacy exhibited her negative attitude toward her with a verbal assault. In a reciprocal manner, disrespect for disrespect, Heidi shouted back at her daughter. Now the dance of disrespect is in motion. By the time Heidi dropped Stacy off at school, neither was pleasant or happy with each other. Both wanted distance. The dance of disrespect always ends in distance. Sadly, as I described earlier, either one of them could have avoided this.

Step Two: Stepping on Each Other's Toes

Nothing worse in a dance than your partner stepping on your toes. Makes you look bad, right? In the dance of disrespect, stepping on toes is a fight for control over the direction and outcome of the conflict. Basically, it's a power struggle. Power exists whenever two people come into contact. How individuals manage power determines the quality of the relationship. Power has several elements, depending on the situation. Let's look at the power dynamics in the encounter Heidi had with Stacy.

The first thing to notice is geography. Space. Heidi enters Stacy's room. Stacy's bedroom is her domain, at least in her mind. On the other hand, Heidi owns the house, including the bedroom. To whom does the power tip in this environment? It depends on respect. Without mutual respect, even the space is a battle for power. Think about what Brandon said to his mother when she entered his bedroom.

"Get the f$%* out of my room!"

Power also involves roles and ranking. What is the role of the parent? Stacy may conclude that a mother exists to meet her needs. Heidi may believe a mother exists to raise her daughter to be a caring and respectful adult.

What about the role of the daughter? Heidi might believe the role of her daughter is to be responsible. Stacy might think she is entitled to have the things she needs and her mother is responsible to deliver.

In terms of ranking, Heidi may think she outranks her daughter because she is her mother. This was clear to many of us growing up in families. However, many adolescents believe they have higher ranking than their parents. Surprised? Listen to the manner in which many young people talk to their parents. When Heidi does not deliver the goods, Stacy is irate because her demands are not met.

The confrontation of power in the morning became a toe-stepping dance for control over the conflict. Stacy blames her mother. Heidi yells back at her daughter. In a fight for control, the two tromp on each other's toes, determined to lead. It is a painful exercise, ending in withdrawal and pain.

Step Three: Avoiding Your Partner.

Throbbing toes would make one exit the dance floor. Family members who step on each other's toes will eventually avoid each other to maintain some semblance of peace, perhaps a false sense of security. *All is well. At least we are not fighting. Besides, why would I be around someone who doesn't respect me?*

Perhaps this is why Kevin gave up on Brandon. Tired of fighting and fearing his anger will get out of control, Kevin retreats from Brandon's oppositional behavior. Now he avoids Brandon and leaves the battle for Heidi to fight. On rare occasions, usually at the prodding of Heidi,

Kevin will get involved, but it never ends well. Father and son attack each other with cutting words, expletives, and mockery.

Kevin calls his son a loser

Brandon says, "Like father like son."

Sadly, Brandon sees his dad as a coward, too weak to man up and be the father he needs.

Avoiding or ignoring a family member is a harmful display of disrespect. It conveys the message that as far as I'm concerned, you don't matter to me anymore. You don't exist. Married couples can coexist in a household and barely say a word to each other during the day. They may pretend to get along in front of the kids, yet dislike or in some cases, despise each other inwardly. A chill pervades the marriage. Couples enter a cold war, keeping up appearances for the sake of the children. Behind the mask, their sentiment toward each other seethes, setting them up for the next issue they can bring to the dance floor.

The dance of respect is different. Rather than taking a defensive, self-protective stance, partners are instructed to begin the dance with a more open posture, inviting their partner to join them in a respectful exchange. The outcome of this dance is closeness, not distance. Let's take a closer look at the steps that make us well.

The 6-Step Dance Of Respect

Step One: Rehearsing Your Approach

This initial step is critical, because it will set the tone for the dance. This involves head and heart preparation. To shift from a reactive to responsive mode, each partner in the dance must slow things down and mentally rehearse a few things: outcome, attitude, and approach. First is outcome.[1] Steven Covey, in his groundbreaking book, *The Seven Habits of Highly Effective People*, highlights the importance of beginning with the end in mind. If your outcome is to win an argument, then you are only thinking about yourself. You may win the argument but lose the respect of your partner. Approaches that seek mutually satisfying out-

---

1 Seven Habits of Highly Effective People, 1989, Free Press

comes generally end well. If individuals can begin by envisioning what their partner needs, they will be in a good posture to begin the dance.

Second, checking your attitude and modifying accordingly will also help. Our brains are designed with interacting systems that regulate thoughts, feelings, and actions. If you have a negative attitude going into an encounter, it will likely elicit a defensive, reactive response from your partner. Therefore, appraisal of attitude and emotions will inform you of what you need to modify before you engage your partner. For example, if you are angry at your partner and feel like you want to yell or give them a piece of your mind, it will serve you well to bring down the intensity of your anger before you begin talking.

I encourage my clients to do a quick self-check-in to note what needs to be modified and to gain better self-control by slowing things down. *Be mad, but don't be bad with your mad.* In other words, don't suppress your feelings; simply regulate the temperature before you express them. If your anger is hot, taking ten deep breaths is a good strategy. Breathing from the diaphragm for five seconds, holding for two, and slowly releasing for another five seconds is an effective deep breathing approach. This simple exercise activates the thinking part of the brain to cool down the feeling part of the brain.

Once you get these two parts of the brain in harmony, your attitude will shift from *attack* to *approach* mode. The approach element preps the mind to do three things: speak carefully, listen openly, and respond respectfully. With this posture set, the partners are ready for step two.

Step Two: Receiving Your Partner

With a right attitude, you are now ready to receive your partner. This means presenting a posture of respect. Receiving your partner involves seeing the person as one deserving affirmation and honor. It requires shifting your view of them from *adversary* to *ally*. In a family, it means viewing your spouse as the person you choose to share life with, or your teenager as one who needs help to navigate the turbulence of adolescence. Remember, the person in your conflict most often wants it resolved too! If you can see them as an ally with you against the problem, you will likely show them respect when you begin the dialogue.

When I work with clients in conflict, I help them to shift from the adversarial position to an alliance by making the problem the problem, instead of the partner the problem. In other words, I help them see that they both want resolution, but they are going about it the wrong way.

Let's return to Kevin and Heidi. One of their constant fights is over parenting. Heidi blames the problems with the kids on Kevin's lack of involvement, coupled with no backup when she needs his support. Kevin complains that Heidi is too uptight as a parent and overreacts to problems with the kids. Notice their postures. They're adversaries attacking each other.

The goal is to get them from being competitors to partners. We point to the positive elements each brings to parenting, the moves they can learn from each other. For example, Heidi's uptightness is her concern for the wellbeing of the kids. If Kevin were to get more involved, Heidi would not think as though it was up to her to keep the children in line.

On the other side, if Heidi could reframe Kevin's disinterest as maintaining a calm attitude and would not overreact but ask for Kevin's help in a stressful situation, perhaps his calm demeanor could diffuse the conflict. By working as partners, seeing the good each brings and blending it, the Hughes would infuse respect into the family culture and their kids would likely alter their behavior.

The point here is that to do the dance of respect, you have to be open to looking at your partner differently. This is not always an easy posture to take, especially when years of resentment have built up. However, you have to start somewhere. Being willing to see the good and open to their point of view will help you master the second step.

Step Three: Respecting The Space Between You

Dance partners have to respect space. In relationships, the same principle holds true in both a literal and figurative sense. In a disrespectful conflict, people are likely to invade each other's space in a variety of ways: getting too close, finger pointing, hitting, blocking doors, or entering rooms uninvited. If you want to have a respectful conversation with another person, you must not violate their space.

Proxemics, the study of space between people, suggests that about eighteen inches is the normal distance in personal relationships and this can vary depending on factors of safety and cohesion. When conflict flares up between people, the space between them will likely lengthen until the matter is resolved. In the Dance of Respect, partners honor the space between them and will not move closer without a cue from their partner.

Tension leads to violations of space. A parent bursts into a teenager's bedroom uninvited. A teenager takes money or a cellphone out without permission.

In what is called a pursuer-withdrawer dynamic, one partner will try to keep communication going, while the other is shutting down. It often leads to the withdrawer leaving the room and the pursuer following. They both want resolution of the conflict, but they go about it in opposite ways.

The pursuer-withdrawer method does not work. It stokes the conflict and creates more animosity between the two. I'll address this pattern more in the chapter on couples. Suffice it to say, when a person in a conflict withdraws, the best thing to do is give them space. On the other hand, it is important for the person needing space to return and try to work things out with their partner once they have a better grip on their emotions. If not, people stockpile their conflicts and use them as ammunition in future arguments.

Step Four: Responding to Your Partner

Remember: In a dance of disrespect, partners react to each other. A snide remark by a teenager is likely followed by a harsh retort. However, in the dance of respect, reactions to conflict are not an option. Instead, partners adopt a deliberate, responsive demeanor. Reactions are impulsive and emotionally charged. Responses are slower and more thoughtful, keeping the emotions in check.

A dance of respect, might feature a snide remark by a teenager, for example:

"I am not going to clean my room."

The parent would follow with a calm, authoritative response:

"You can choose not to clean your room, but you forfeit your chance to go out with your friends tonight. Is this what you want to do? Or do you want to rethink?"

Here, the parent does not get baited into a power struggle by respecting the teenager's need for autonomy, the power to choose. At the same time, the parent remains the final authority without losing control and being reactive. Disarming a power struggle with a teenager will likely lead to a more controlled and responsive dialog. It may take your teen some time to join you in a respectful talk if the pattern of disrespect has been your dance for a long time. As a parent, you have to take the lead and maintain the position of respect for a while until the pattern breaks and the dance shifts into a mutually respectful routine.

Practicing the dance of respect, listening skills heighten. Responses slow down and become more thoughtful. The ability to think about things from your partner's position improves, giving both people a heightened understanding of where each other is coming from, leading to more effective communication and stronger connection. When this pattern emerges, the partners can move into the next step, repairing conflict.

Step Five: Repairing Mistakes

Mistakes, mess-ups, blunders. Whatever you label them, expect them when learning a new dance. Is it any different in life? As an educator, I supervise counseling students in their practicum and internship programs. In this setting, I give them feedback about the counseling skills I've observed in their work with clients. It amazes me how often students will make comments like, "I should have known this" or "I can't believe I made this mistake." I chuckle whenever I hear this because the implication suggests that they should not make mistakes. Early in their training, I normalize mistake-making. It is inevitable. In fact, no matter how proficient one becomes in anything, they will still make mistakes.

In relationships, partners make mistakes. Things are said or done that cause conflict or inflict harm. Most often, the harm is not intentional. The key is learning how to repair mistakes and learn from them so the behavior doesn't repeat and patterns don't form. The beauty in the dance of respect is it helps people do the one thing they find most difficult in relationships, resolve conflict and repair harm. Later, I will walk you through a process that helps partners repair conflict in a manner that brings resolution, builds respect, and enhances the relational bond. For now, let's highlight the last step in the dance of respect.

Step 6: The Rhythm of Reciprocity

Dance involves rhythm. Partners move in syncopation to the music.

It's the rhythm of reciprocity. To reciprocate simply means to respond in like manner to how a person acts toward you. If your partner is attempting to repair a conflict, the reciprocal response would be to join in the repair process. Reciprocation can also alleviate the possibility of conflict. Let's take a look at how Heidi and her daughter Stacy got into a rhythm of reciprocation.

Heidi knocks on Stacy's door in the morning before school.

HEIDI
"Good morning, Stace. May I come in?"

STACY
"Yeah, come on in."

HEIDI
"You look a little frustrated. Something wrong?"

STACY
"I am frustrated. My new outfit is still in the dirty clothes bin. I told you I was out of hair gel. Did you forget to pick some up yesterday?"

HEIDI
"Yesterday was a crazy day for me. I ended up working late and I couldn't get to the store. I don't recall you asking me to wash your outfit."

STACY
"I thought I asked you. Maybe I didn't. This is awful, Mom. What am I going to do? Katie bought a new outfit and is wearing it to impress Ethan. She knows I like him. I can't believe this is happening to me."

HEIDI
"I can see you're upset. I'll tell you what: Why don't you wear this combo?" She hands her a top and pants from her closet. "You looked great in it when you wore it to your cousin's last week. If you get ready quickly, we can pick up the gel on the way to school.

STACY
"Okay. Thanks. By the way, can you drive me and some friends to the mall after school?"

HEIDI
"Sorry, Stace. I still have to shop and get dinner ready. You can ask your father, but just remember to be home at six.

STACY
"Never mind. Besides, Dad never wants to do anything after work."

Notice, no reactive pattern. Heidi handles her daughter's frustration without being defensive. She validates Stacy's feelings and shifts to problem-solving. The more Heidi adopts this posture with her daughter, the more likely Stacy will reciprocate. Keep in mind, in the early stages of the dance, a partner may not always respond to the respectful cue, especially if you have been in a pattern of conflict for some time. It will take patience and consistency to develop the pattern of healthy reciprocity. Someone has to initiate, and in a parent-teen relationship, parents should lead.

As you can see, the dance of respect has double the amount of steps than the dance of disrespect. Why? Because disrespect is reactive and self-protective. Respect slows interactions down, allowing a person to gain composure and think through their approach. Thus, they are able to balance their own needs with the needs of the other person. Their partner is less likely to be defensive and more open to reciprocate with respect. The result is the resolution of conflict, mutual respect, and increased harmony.

Self-respect is often a missing element in interpersonal relationships. Most of us would like to think we respect ourselves, but our interpersonal problems show we don't. Consequently, individuals lacking personal boundaries allow others to treat them without honor. This brings serious harm not only to the relationship, but to the self-identity of the person who allows this behavior. Before we work on bringing respect back in our relationships, let's focus on bringing self-respect back.

Chapter Three

Bringing Self-Respect Back

Dancing Solo

> *"It takes a lifetime to learn how to be able to hold your own ground, to go out to others, to be open to them without losing your ground. And to hold your ground without shutting others out."* — Martin Buber

Heidi parks the car in the company lot, shuts off the engine, and pulls down the vanity mirror to adjust her makeup after the tearful exchange with Stacy earlier this morning. Taking time to gain her composure before she enters her next battle zone, Heidi wonders why she tries so hard yet gets so little in return. Not only does she feel disrespected in her marriage and family, but on the job Heidi encounters a work environment that undervalues her.

As a branch manager of a local bank, Heidi carries many responsibilities. Like her husband, she feels the squeeze between the expectations of upper management and the employees she supervises. While she feels confident in her ability to lead her employees, Heidi's biggest challenge is the lack of support she receives from her boss. He has no problem reducing his workload by adding more to hers. Heidi, the consummate people-pleaser, takes on the added responsibility without complaint, even if it means working extra hours or bringing work home. Her boss is also aware of her talents and views her as a potential threat to his position. Consequently, he takes credit for her work while finding things to criticize. Not wanting to jeopardize her job security, Heidi absorbs the complaints, vowing to work harder so he cannot find anything to attack.

What's even more troubling for Heidi is that she feels like she has no one to confide in about her problems. When she tries to talk to Kevin, he tells her to suck it up, or points out her faults and lectures her on what she could have done to avoid the problem. Kevin, the master coper, uses one routine to deal with stress. He retires to the gazebo in the backyard with a bud in one hand and a Bud in the other. Smoking weed and having a beer is the perfect remedy for his problems. He can escape the pressures of work and home by becoming comfortably numb.

Heidi, on the other hand, tried numbing her pain but it only made things worse. A stress eater, she found that weight gain made her more stressed out. She decided to join the health club and began her own routine of weekly exercise. Before long, Heidi met Tom, a guy in her Pilates class who took an interest in her. At first, it seemed innocent, just some small talk about the class and a few of the weird characters who seem out-of-step. Heidi noticed that she and Tom always ended up working out together and lingering at the health bar. She liked how Tom made her laugh and listened when she talked about her frustrations at work. Finally, Heidi found someone who understood her, did not criticize her, or use her for that matter.

One day at work, Heidi's boss was especially harsh toward her, to the point of tears. She retreated to her office and called Tom. His calming tone and reassuring voice was what she needed to regain her composure. He suggested they meet for lunch at a nearby park. Without a second thought, Heidi agreed to meet Tom. An hour lunch turned into an afternoon affair at a nearby hotel. Heidi didn't care about work, her boss, or her husband. All she cared about at that moment was being with someone who could fill her inner longing. Later she would worry about the repercussions, if any, from her absence from the office. For now, she rested comfortably in the arms of a man she felt cared for her.

For weeks, Heidi and Tom continued to meet. Heidi had the best of both worlds. Not only was Tom a great listener, but he was good in bed. She felt really alive for the first time in a long time. While she felt some guilt about being unfaithful in her marriage, Heidi justified her choice because it didn't seem Kevin cared about her anyway. Besides, Tom knew how to satisfy her needs and she wasn't going to give this up. Heidi didn't know where this relationship was going, but she wanted to enjoy it.

After about a month, Heidi noticed Tom acting differently. At first she dismissed it, thinking he was having a bad day, but then it seemed as though a pattern was forming. She noticed fewer texts. Heidi was initiating more of the contact. When they did talk, Tom was not as attentive as he was in the past. Furthermore, he was not going to the Pilates class as frequently. At times, he seemed disinterested in Heidi and even annoyed in conversation. Soon, he started taking interest in another woman at the health club. Heidi had this sinking, all too familiar feeling that she had been used again. Tom was no different from her boss or Kevin. In the end, it was all about him. Heidi was even more alone and depressed.

Unfortunately, this scenario is repeated daily. I hear it all the time. It is a sad and painful reality for many who become vulnerable only to be crushed by someone they trusted to care for them. Compounded disrespect. In the case of Heidi, she was disrespected by her husband, children, and boss. She thought she found it in Tom, but was sadly mistaken. On a deeper level, Heidi lost her self-respect.

We hear a lot about self-respect, but what does it mean? How does one really know when one has it? I picture self-respect like a diamond with many facets. When exposed to light, the various hues of the color spectrum are radiant. Like that diamond, self-respect is a precious asset that requires special attention. In essence, self-respect is about how we see and care for ourselves. Simply put, it's me taking care of me. I will highlight three facets of self-respect: self-acceptance, self-care, and self-responsibility.

Self-Acceptance: I'm Okay With Me

One of the key facets of self-respect is self-acceptance. It's the ability to look at yourself in the mirror and say, *I'm okay with me*. Self-acceptance embraces strengths and imperfections as a way of life and does not get trapped into having to keep it all together to feel good about oneself. This is not easy for some people who are encoded with a perfectionism gene. People who mistakenly believe they have to be perfect to be accepted set themselves up for failure. For these individuals, self-acceptance is one bar-raising pole vault after another. They never enjoy the jump. Instead, they feel relief for clearing the bar they set up in their heads.

Often, when individuals come to counseling I write the following statements on a marker board:

I'm not a perfect person.
We are not a perfect couple.
We are not a perfect family.
I am not a perfect counselor.

This opens a dialogue that is disarming to the self-protective armor many wear, thinking there must be something wrong with them if they are not perfect.

Self-acceptance acknowledges imperfection but doesn't efface the value of the person. Rather, it enhances personal value because others feel relaxed around individuals who are comfortable with themselves. I am fascinated by how powerful connections are made when people are real with one another. We are drawn to people who are honest about their struggles, deal with them, yet don't take themselves too seriously. These are people who know how to relax with themselves and others without feeling like they have to perform.

Parents can help their children develop a healthy self-identity by being more real with their kids about their own shortcomings and by owning up to their mistakes. Often, children believe they are loved only when they meet their parents' expectations. Whether this is instilled or imagined, parents must be aware of this vulnerability and separate children from their behavior.

When I was raising my children, I often reflected on the biblical story of the baptism of Jesus to remind myself how to keep things in perspective as a dad. In the Jordan River, Jesus heard these words from his heavenly father: *"This is my son whom I love. With him I am well pleased."*

I like how he sequenced his compliments. First, he spoke to his unconditional love for his son. Second, he complimented his behavior.

Sometimes we are not pleased with our children's behavior. However, does that mean we don't love them? Of course not. Yet how often is the truth obscured by our reactions to misbehavior? Showing disapproval, speaking harshly, and criticizing our kids by pointing out their faults can lead them to think they are not loved. Before long, they will begin to think they are unlovable and will struggle with self-acceptance. Much of the oppositional behavior parents experience from their kids is based on resentment stemming from a deeper belief that they don't measure up to their parents' expectations.

Sadly, many base parenting on notions of perfection. Undercurrents of guilt and fear often propel parenting. I will address this more in the chapter on bringing respect back into your family. Suffice it to say that parents can model self-acceptance by becoming more comfortable with their imperfections and putting less pressure on themselves and their children.

Not only is self-acceptance based on acknowledging imperfections, but it includes embracing the positive qualities and traits that define us as individuals. I often ask clients to list their positive and negative traits in two separate columns. In many cases, a client will easily fill the column of negative attributes and struggle to list positive qualities. This indicates that we tend to focus more on the negative than the positive—what's wrong versus what's right about us. When our thoughts are weighted to the negative side, we lower our self-esteem and negatively skew our self-identity.

Accuracy is a key to a healthy picture of oneself. If you struggle filling the positive column, perhaps you can ask people you trust to give you feedback on what they like about you. Ask them to identify your positive traits and what makes you a valued person in their life. To get an accurate view, you may also ask for input on your negative traits as well. You might be surprised to discover they don't have as many things to list on the negative side as you do. Perhaps they may state that you are too hard on yourself, deflect praise, and take on more than you can handle.

Self-acceptance is easier to embrace when we understand that we are a work in progress. We do not have to wait until we've reached some level of achievement or success before we accept ourselves. Rather, we can accept ourselves every day as individuals on a journey of discovery, growth, and possibility.

Personally, by coming to terms with who I am, I have learned how to accept each day as a gift and an opportunity to grow. I feel comfortable in my own skin. I am okay with me.

My spiritual values also play a vital role in my self-acceptance. I believe God accepts me where I am and for who I am. It is unconditional love and acceptance. This frees me up to look at myself the way God does. The growth and change I want to experience is not solely up to me, but God plays a role as well.[2] A guiding verse in my life says, *"He who began a good work in you will carry it on until the day of completion."* God sees all my imperfections and all my positive traits. He doesn't wait until I get my act together before he gives his approval. If God is this honest and generous in his vision of me, then it makes sense for me to take on this vision of myself.

Self-Care: I Matter

Another facet in self-respect is self-care, a core belief in the inherent value of one's individuality and right to existence. Often, we take our right to existence for granted, but how much thought and effort do we give to living a full life? Life is a gift and we have no guarantee how long it will last. Therefore, it would make sense to get the most out of life by taking good care of ourselves and investing time and energy into things that promote healthy living. Care of self is synonymous with respect of self.

In the initial phase of my work with individuals on marriage or parenting issues, I assess each person's level of self-care. I want to know what they do to fill their personal tank. This personal tank comprises elements of the intellect, the emotions, the body, and the spirit. Why do I start with self-care? My approach is simple: *"A healthy me translates into a better we."* Here's the progression. First, take care of yourself and you will be a healthy partner in marriage. Next, as a couple you invest in your marriage, you will be healthy parents for your kids. The net result is your kids will feel secure and function more appropriately under your care and influence. Unfortunately, in our culture, the pyramid is inverted. Parents are over-focused on their kids, which leaves little time and energy for marriage and self-care. Exhausted, depleted of energy, and with little time to spare, many retreat to the TV remote or laptop where they can zone out until they pass out and go to bed.

Self-care is unique to every person because it is an expression of your individuality. It is your dance with yourself, doing things you enjoy. This

---

2   Holy Bible - Book of Philippians 1:6

became more clear to me this morning before I began writing. My wife and I are staying at a beautiful resort in Riviera Maya. After a sunrise walk and light breakfast, we decided to hit the health club for workout. While going through our individual routines we were transfixed on a woman in her mid-twenties running on the treadmill. For me, the treadmill is a boring exercise, but I began to have second thoughts as I watched this woman run, skip, jump, do the grapevine, twirl, and move her arms in an amazing dance routine. Before long, several people were watching her exercise, moving fluidly, yet at a rigorous pace. Once she finished her exercise, my wife was eager to ask the young woman about her routine. We learned that she is both a dancer and an assistant trainer to a famous exercise trainer. Talking to the young woman, it became clear to me that her dance and exercise routine was an expression of her winsome personality.

Self-care is largely an expression of self. It requires you to be a student of you. Do you know yourself? Do you know what you like? What you don't like? What gives you energy when you do it? Intellectually, I enjoy reading, learning, and discovery. When I returned to school in my early forties, I discovered an affinity with the academic environment. Perhaps this is why I jumped at the opportunity to return to my alma mater to join the faculty as a lecturer in the graduate program. Physically, I am at home in a health club. Now in my fifties, my weekly routine remains 2-3 days each of full-court basketball—my addiction—and core training. When I am out of my routine, I feel sluggish, irritable at times, and not centered.

To connect with myself emotionally, I journal, listen to music, spend time in nature, and watch movies that evoke emotions. Socially, apart from time with family, I enjoy hanging with the guys at the health club, or my compadres in a business owners group. Finally, spirituality is my deepest connection with myself. Here, I spend time with my Maker reading, praying, and listening. The profound elements of my faith shape my character and remind me of how deeply and unconditionally I am loved by God.

How about you? What do you currently do to connect you with yourself? What would you like to add? My bucket list includes dance lessons, skydiving, and learning to speak a second language. Try choosing one thing to enjoy. If this is something you are not accustomed to, then start with something easy. Why not write it down now and put today's date and time next to it? Now, set a time of completion and write it beneath todays' date. Lastly, write the following statement and fill in the blank:

I give myself permission to _____ *as my promise to take care of me.*

All that's left is taking action on the promise you made to yourself.

Earlier this week, I met with a couple as a follow-up to a previous session where I prescribed a stress reducing and relaxing activity for the wife. The Rx was a tough one for her because of her superwoman proclivity to put everyone and everything before herself. Yet, in this session, before she even spoke, I knew she had completed her assignment by simply observing her countenance. I commented on her demeanor and she replied, "I followed through on my promise to do something for myself."

"What did you do?" I asked.

"I went to a day spa and had a massage" she said.

My curiosity led me to ask, "What did you notice differently about yourself afterward?"

Here, my client listed several benefits personally and interpersonally from the time she invested in herself.

After she reported that it has been two years since she had a massage, I asked, "How long will it be next time?".

When she said, "I'd like to go next week," her husband said, "If it will de-stress you, I'll buy you weekly massages!"

Knowing the couple could afford it, I urged them to follow through on the agreement.

Self-care motivates you to think more respectfully about yourself and how you live. When my clients make the excuse that they want to do more for themselves but don't have the time, I challenge their way of thinking. The reality is we invest our time and treasure in the things that matter. Kids matter. Work matters. Others matter. It's high time for you to matter. When you shift your priorities to emphasize self-respect, you will not make excuses. You'll feel empowered to take care of yourself.

Taking Care of the Intruders

While there is much more I can write about self-care, there is one aspect I want to address because I find it a common problem with many individuals I see in counseling. I call them the intruders.

Intruders are conditions individuals have that interfere in the quality of their lives and interpersonal relationships. In mental health, they are classified as disorders: mood disorders, anxiety-based disorders, and thought disorders, to name a few. Individuals who live with one of these conditions have to contend with the intrusive nature of the symptoms. In the case of anxiety, the dynamic features include extreme worry, cyclical thinking, overanalyzing, imagining worst-case scenarios, and a need for control. Managing anxiety becomes a challenge because this condition has both neurological and environmental components.

Intruders like anxiety create problems to one degree or another, depending on how individuals respond to the intrusion. When clients see me, they are often unaware they have an intruder contributing to their problems. All they know is that they cannot relax, worry too much about things, and need to control. Once I identify the intruder, I make the client aware of its presence. We process how the intruder causes them problems. This psycho-educational process informs them of the symptoms and features of their condition. They begin to separate themselves from the problem.

Next, I offer them a choice: "Either you manage your intruder or your intruder will manage you." The purpose here is to stress the importance of developing coping strategies that reduce the frequency and intensity of the condition.

Identifying intruders in relationship counseling has both a disarming and empowering effect. It is disarming because it shifts individuals from fighting each other to joining forces in battle against the intruder. It is empowering because the individuals work together to manage the intruder, a strategy that results in a decrease in conflict and an increase in connection. Externalizing the problem escapes the tendency to pathologize individuals and it preserves their dignity. Furthermore, it raises the level of compassion in the family and increases cooperation. Family members reorganize their interactions to keep the intruder from holding them hostage in a negative pattern of communication.

Using "code word" is often a good way of externalizing an intruder, say depression for example. The word "submarine" can be a code word for depression. If a spouse notices her husband is more moody, irritable and distant she might say, "It appears the submarine has descended below the surface. What do you think?" The husband might reply, "Yeah, I would agree. It's just below the surface, not too far." The couple can have a short dialog to talk about how to handle it so it doesn't become too intrusive in their day.

Perhaps as you are reading this, you realize that you have an intruder in your life. I highlighted anxiety and depression as examples, but for others it could be ADD (Attention-Deficit Disorder), PTSD (Post-Traumatic Stress Disorder), OCD (Obsessive-Compulsive Disorder), or a physical intruder like chronic pain, multiple sclerosis, or some other medical condition. Maybe you've become hard on yourself or others, thinking you or they are the problem. Could it be that the real culprit is an intruder? This is not to say that all problems boil down to one cause. Sometimes, our problems are due to wrong choices. This is obvious. On the other hand, when an intruder like depression or PTSD is present, it will wreak havoc in your life if you don't do something about it.

If an element of self-respect is self-care, then it makes sense to address all health issues: physical, mental, and emotional. The old stigma surrounding mental health has been debunked in our era, so increasingly individuals are seeking professional help to treat these conditions. If you have an intruder you are not currently addressing, I encourage you to seek professional help to learn how to manage the condition so that it does not manage you. Also, if you notice an intruder causing a rift in your marriage or your family, then reach out for help. These are manageable problems if you seek the right kind of assistance. By doing so, you show respect for yourself and others will respect you as well.

Self-Responsibility: I Can Manage My Life

A third element in self-respect is taking responsibility—managing your life. Personal responsibility is not as highly valued in our culture today as it was in previous generations. Instead, we place more emphasis on rights, entitlements, and freedom. What we often see is unbridled, impulse-driven behavior without ownership of outcome. Read the headlines and see the evidence. Ponzi schemes, performance-enhancing drugs in professional sports, cheating, lying, stealing, and murder all masked by cover-ups and blame.

When the outcome brings negative consequences, individuals are more likely to assign blame than to accept responsibility. For example, children blame parents for missing assignments because the parents did not ask them if they had homework. How about a spouse who blames an affair on the other because of a lack of romance in their marriage? On a larger scale, blame seems to be the strategy between political parties who seem unwilling to bear responsibility for contributing to the debt crisis, flattened economy, or high rate of unemployment.

Rights without responsibility is a disturbing trend in adolescent-to-adult transitions. It appears that young adults are eager to flex their independence when it comes to the rights of adulthood, but are more than willing to delegate the responsibilities to their parents. They enjoy the freedom of using cell phones, driving cars, and making purchases with a credit card. However, they have no qualms letting their parents pay the bills. Many young adults also struggle managing the responsibilities and expectations of work. Employers complain about the lack of work ethic, high absenteeism, and unrealistic expectations young adults exhibit. They give their employers fits when they routinely call off work because something more important comes along. I will address this matter further in the chapter on parents and children.

The dance of self-respect adds personal responsibility to the routine. If you want to have self-respect then you have to take ownership of your life and be responsible for the choices you make. It includes considering how your decisions will affect not only you, but others as well. In counseling ethics, we use the term non-maleficence, which means *avoiding doing harm* to clients. It's counterpart is beneficence, *doing good* for our clients. These virtues guide our conduct. The bottom line is protecting the welfare of our clients. I recommend you follow these principles in how you govern yourself. Self-responsibility is about your personal welfare, avoiding doing harm to yourself, and doing what is good for you.

For example, let's see how this applies to Heidi, the wife, mother, and career woman who felt disrespected in her roles and sought comfort in the arms of another man. Clearly, Heidi is a woman who bears much responsibility for others. She exhibits benevolent behavior in her care-taking roles, and avoids doing harm in the process. She strives to be good toward others in a kind, loving, and respectful manner.

The problem is not how Heidi treats people; it is in how she treats herself. Heidi has low self-respect, so she allows others to treat her with disrespect. Moreover, she lacks healthy boundaries in her personal relationships. Consequently, people take advantage of her and criticize her without reprisal. One might add that Heidi lacks the skills of assertion to stand up for herself and be clear with others on how she expects to be treated. Instead, she bites her lip and works harder, hoping to gain approval and avoid criticism.

Self-respect has a built-in mechanism that is triggered when personal boundaries are violated. Call it a gut check. It alerts the voice to speak with authority and inform others that they have crossed a line that will not be tolerated. There is a poignant moment in the movie, *The King's Speech,* where King George is expressing his displeasure at his speech coach because he wrongfully sat on the monarch's throne. When repeatedly challenged by the coach about his argument, the king shouts, "Because I have a voice!"

If you want the respect of others, you have to find your voice and express it to people so they know where you stand and how you expect to be treated. Furthermore, you must hold your ground so others know you are serious. In my work as a relational communication specialist, I help clients find their voice. When this happens, it is a beautiful thing to behold. Individuals are empowered, in some cases for the first time in their lives, to speak honestly and openly about what they are thinking and feeling, while making their needs known.

Heidi struggled being assertive and on occasions when she did use her voice, she screamed and felt out of control. For the most part, Heidi kept things on the inside and buried her hurt. Eventually, the emotional pain made her vulnerable to someone who would listen, validate her feelings, and offer the warmth of physical touch she longed for. Sadly, the man she had an affair with also used her and left when it was convenient for him. It is easy to feel sorry for Heidi and blame the people in her life. Certainly, there is cause for this. However, Heidi's choices were a big part of the problem as well. First of all, she was not acting benevolently toward herself; she was not doing what was good for her by allowing others to treat her so poorly. Furthermore, she acted with self-malfeasance, doing harm to herself by trying to cure her pain in an affair. Although she found temporary relief, she put herself at risk personally and interpersonally.

For the most part, affairs are complex and risky. The complexity of infidelity is in managing two separate worlds. In an affair, individuals experience the intoxicating, seductive elixir of passion, romance, adventure, emotional connection, and perhaps the thrill of being naughty. This is in stark contrast to the real world at home with expectations, responsibilities, and endless work, offering little or no appreciation, constant criticism, and a lack of affection. This daily ritual leaves one feeling empty and longing for connection. The avoidance of marital pain triggers the need for connection and a dose of passion as a remedy. The pattern of orbiting two worlds is set in motion.

Exposure, of course, is the obvious risk. Managing two worlds is not sustainable over the long haul, except in rare cases. For most people, however, the affair happens in proximity to the marital world: coworker, neighbor, common friend, Facebook, or relative. The impact of exposure and collateral damage is extensive, in most cases altering the lives of family members forever. Typically, the newfound love in the affair cannot survive the pain and suffering inflicted upon oneself and others in the process.

Having counseled several clients during and after an affair, I have found common responses. Many have told me that they never pictured themselves being in an affair. In fact, they describe it as a surreal experience, as if they were talking about someone else: *I'm not the kind of person who would do something like this.* However, the reality of the affair also leaves some feeling a profound sense of guilt and shame. *What's wrong with me? What kind of person would do this to their family? I'm so selfish. You must think I'm a horrible person.* Self-deprecation is compounded by feelings of emptiness and anger. *I experienced a connection I've been missing for such a long time. Why did it have to happen this way?*

In counseling, we unpack the factors that contributed to the affair and begin the process of helping the person regain the key element underlying all others, their self-respect. My goal in working with individuals is helping them get their self-respect back by focusing on self-acceptance, self-care, and self-responsibility. Through this process, clients find their voice, establish healthy boundaries, manage their health, and make better choices for themselves. The net gain is clarity about self-identity, knowing who they are, what they want, and where they want to go in life. Furthermore, their relationships shift to function in a respectful manner. By establishing clear boundaries, others are more likely to show them respect. Those who are unwilling to show respect no longer remain in the close circle of contact.

Where You Are And Where To Go From Here

As you come to the end of this chapter, how do you see yourself when it comes to self-respect? Do you have a healthy sense of self-acceptance or do you constantly criticize yourself for your perceived imperfections? How well do you do in self-care? Do you take time for yourself to do things that improve the overall quality of your life and nourish your soul? Are you managing the intruders in your life or simply tolerating them? How about the area of self-responsibility? Are you taking responsibility for your life and the choices you make? Are you doing good or harm to yourself in the choices you make to deal with the problems in your life? Do you blame others? Do you constantly blame yourself for things others do to you?

The dance of self-respect is solo. It focuses on you. Be clear on who you are, your interests, beliefs, values, and style. Be clear in communicating how you want others to act toward you. This includes advocating for your right to be treated with respect and dignity. Bringing self-respect back in your life begins with establishing boundaries *for* yourself and *with* others.

Step One: Boundaries for Me
You may be nodding your head in agreement, yet wondering how to do it. Easier said than done, right? True. Perhaps you have taken the first step by reading this book. The next step for you is to take a quick inventory of your life and decide what you are doing to yourself that is no longer acceptable. This might be a negative belief or habit based on this belief that causes you harm because you don't like how it makes you feel toward yourself. Begin with something relatively easy and doable. Stop rejecting compliments or finding fault with yourself. Decide that

when others compliment you, you will kindly thank them. Commit not to point out your flaws publicly, and instead try to say something positive about yourself.

Are you doing something you know is not good for you? Is it causing or putting you at risk for harm? It may bring temporary relief or fill a void but in the end will inflict pain. Making excuses or justifying the behavior is only a means of avoiding the risk of harm you face. The consequences will only make your life harder than it is right now. Pause. Think. Consider the risk you are taking. Do something now to address this problem. Waiting too long may be too late. *Setting boundaries for me* means setting limits on yourself.

Boundaries includes scheduling time for yourself to do the self-care activities that will fill your tank. Today I'm writing from my hotel room in San Francisco where I am enjoying two days of personal time while my wife attends a seminar. Later in the week we will enjoy a day or two in Napa Valley. In the past, I would have decided to stay home and see more clients. However, I have learned to invest time in *me* so I can contribute to a better *we* in my marriage.

What can you do today to schedule time for yourself? It can be as simple as sitting alone in your yard, eyes closed, listening to the sounds of nature. Is there a class you've wanted to take but never took the time? Finish reading this chapter then sign up for the class. Go ahead, do it! Create some space in your life for you to be with you doing something you want to do.

Step Two: Boundaries with Others

Think about the relationships where you feel most disrespected. Is there a common theme? Do people take advantage of you? Are you criticized or not taken seriously? Do you give more and accept less? Are you prone to give up your needs and give in to theirs? Do you have a hard time saying the word no? If you answered yes to one or more of these questions, you have poor relational boundaries and you likely feel resentful and lonely.

A good place to start in setting boundaries with others is getting acclimated to saying no when presented with a request you are unable to do or do not wish to do. Denying a request is not the end of the world.

Disappointing others because you do not always meet their expectations is normal in human relations. When others disappoint you, do you get over it? Guess what? They will get over it too! If not, then perhaps there is a problem on their end, not yours. Most people get over their disappointments relatively quickly. If you keep this in mind, you are more likely to decline a request and find your true voice with others.

Step Three: Find a Safe Place to Express Yourself

If you have a hard time setting boundaries, you may benefit from finding a place where you can go and rediscover yourself, a safe place where you will not be judged or criticized for using your voice. Some people reconnect with themselves through spirituality, connecting with others in community, perhaps a church setting or support group.

Another means of self-expression is getting involved in an activity—old or new—that resonates with you. It could be something in the arts or music, sports, nature, travel and adventure, a hobby or educational course. Finding something that connects you with yourself will open the channels of self-expression.

Others find their voice in counseling, where self-expression is encouraged. Counselors promote the dignity and welfare of their clients, displaying what Psychologist Carl Rogers described as "unconditional positive regard" toward them. In a safe, nonjudgmental environment emphasizing compassion and support, you can begin a journey of self-discovery.

Step Four: Address Your Needs for and Barriers to Connection

A basic need within all people is human connection. Whether it be in marriage, familial relationships, friendships, or partnerships of some sort, each of us have an innate need to belong and connect with others. This can be tricky to accomplish because of the self-protective patterns of interaction we develop over time. These defense measures provide a safe barrier against potential hurt, but they also limit our ability to form close relationships. While we value the safety of attachment, we also fear rejection, abandonment, or some other response that causes emotional harm. Consequently, self-protective behaviors such as avoidance, conflict, withdrawal, or anger push people away, including times when no real threat exists. This leaves individuals feeling lonely, empty, and vulnerable to getting their intimacy needs met in unhealthy ways.

If you struggle forming healthy sustaining relationships with others, I suggest you address this matter. Attachment needs, basic to human survival, are powerful and can be resistant to change. Unconscious fears related to abandonment, rejection, or defectiveness can emotionally paralyze individuals who want intimacy but are unwilling to risk failure. If you don't address these underlying fears, they will surface in future relationships and possibly sabotage your attempt to form a close connection. For those who have concluded that close relationships are not possible and have given up on forming anything more than casual relationships, I ask you to rethink your position and consider addressing the underlying fears with someone competent to walk you through this process.

Attachment injuries are a casualty of living in an imperfect world with imperfect people. Experiences in relationships throughout life that leave people feeling anxious, unloved, or uncared for form deep wounds and the barriers to meaningful connections and intimate relationships. These emotional wounds can be mended in a safe, secure human attachment that allows individuals to express their fears and vulnerabilities and integrate new beliefs that challenge old ways of thinking. A counseling relationship is the best setting to begin this process of change. I encourage you to start here.

Step Five: Create Margin in Your Life

Is your plate full? No margin for empty space? You're too busy! I know; everyone is busy. Not true. Many people have their calendars maxed out between work, family obligations, and social events. Run, run, run. I hear about it all the time. I have a busy schedule, too, running a practice, seeing clients, teaching at a university, and oh yeah, writing a book. However, if you look at my calendar, you will find margin, room for me to do me stuff or nothing at all. To write this book, I had to schedule blocks of time to write every week. I also booked getaways to give me ample time to rest and write without distractions.

Do you have margin? Is there room in your weekly calendar that has just you penciled in? Bringing self-respect back does require you investing time in self-care activities. So, where will you start? Morning jog? Afternoon swim? Evening walk in the park? How about a spa treatment? That's where I am heading now!

Chapter Four

Bringing Respect Back Into Your Marriage

KEVIN ROLLS IN the driveway after drudging out another day at work. *Only twenty-seven more years of hard labor and I can retire.* Noticing Heidi's car is missing, Kevin braces himself for what he will likely encounter when he enters the house.

As usual, his kids do not disappoint. Brandon has taken over command central, sitting in Kevin's recliner, headphones on, fully engaged in a combat game. Stacy and her three friends retreat to her bedroom, having just evacuated the kitchen. Kevin surveys the environment. Dishes piled in the sink. Trash container overflowing with garbage cascading on the floor. Dirty clothes in piles. A dog begging for someone to fill the food and water bowls. Speaking of food, nothing prepared, no aroma of a home-cooked meal. Just the putrid smell of Brandon's socks tossed on the kitchen table.

After putting up with the demands at work, Kevin is not in the mood to deal with this set of problems. Besides, it's Heidi's fault. She spends too much time at work and the health club. Kevin grabs a beer from the fridge and a bag of weed from his sock drawer and retreats to the gazebo to escape the family drama, leaving it for Heidi to fix.

Checking out leaves Kevin clueless to what's going on around him. His kids don't respect him because he doesn't care enough to take charge. To Brandon, Kevin is the guy who keeps the TV running and supplies the weed he steals. Stacy uses her dad as the go-to parent to get a yes when she knows her mother will say no.

Heidi is also losing respect for Kevin. His obsession with the gazebo is getting old. She is tired of his criticism and loathes his absence in household affairs. When he does get involved, he makes life miserable for her. In the end, it works because she would rather take on the extra burden of household demands than deal with his attitude. Unfortunately, the kids have learned his routine and perform it flawlessly.

Feeling distraught and raw, Heidi returns to the war zone, scans the landscape, and breaks down. Nobody has lifted a finger to help around the home. Once again, she is left alone to clean up the mess and serve dinner. While attending to the dog, Heidi peers through the kitchen window and catches a glimpse of Kevin, enveloped in smoke, facing outward.

Heidi hits her breaking point. Eyes focused, jaw set, she marches into the gazebo and launches a verbal assault her husband cannot escape.

"I quit, Kevin! I'm not going to play this game anymore. Your body is here, but the rest of you is M.I.A.. I might as well be a single parent. If you're going to check out, you might as well move out!"

Marital Drift

What happened to this couple that brought them to a breaking point? I can assure you it didn't happen overnight. Unfortunately, the Hughes suffer a condition I see much too often in couples today. I call it marital drift. It is the slow, subtle distancing that happens when couples are not paying attention to their relationship. Drifting happens so slowly and imperceptibly that you are often not aware until something finally gets your attention.

I remember several years ago when my wife and I were on vacation in Mexico. We tossed our towels on the blue resort chairs, ran across the powder-white sand and jumped into the turquoise waters of the Caribbean Sea. For over an hour, we swam and snorkeled in the water. Finally, we decided to call it quits for the day and headed for the shore. As I looked ahead of me to locate the blue chairs, I noticed they were white. In fact, the resort looked different. Scanning the shore, I found our blue chairs three resorts down from where we stood. While we were preoccupied in the water, the cross-breeze drifted us away from our base.

I think marriages drift when couples are not paying attention. What causes marital drift? One might argue that it happens when one or both partners fall out of love. Another might conclude that perhaps they are not a good match. These points of view have merit in some marriages. However, what I notice more often is that couples drift apart because they are so busy doing other things that they neglect the needs of the relationship. Research shows that marital satisfaction declines after a few years of marriage. This occurs not because couples get bored with each other as much as that they are too busy running this operation called a family that they neglect to invest in the marriage.

Think about it. Relationship satisfaction is high in the early stages of marriage not simply because of the escalated romantic factor, but also because couples have little or no responsibility to other things that compete for attention. Sure, they may have jobs to go to every day, but the after-hours and weekends can be invested in the relationship, going on dates, trips, and just hanging out on the sofa with Netflix. However, when couples take the plunge of commitment, get married, buy a home, and start raising kids, on top of holding down their jobs, they are in full-blown Operation Family.

Managing a family is like owning a business; it is a twenty-four-seven job. Couple interaction shifts to negotiating the family operation: paying bills, cleaning house, driving kids to sporting events, music lessons, play dates. Like owning a business, there are no days off, especially if you have young children. Between work, kids, and managing a house, the tasks are many and the fuel supply low by the time kids are tucked in bed. Most couples I talk to have little or nothing in the tank at the end of the day when they finally have an hour or so of free time. Exhausted after a day of caring for others, they may have enough energy to grab a snack and park themselves in front of the television for some brainless activity or comic relief, perhaps a reality-based TV show that offers a few laughs and reassures them that they are doing okay compared to the Simmons, Kardashians, or Housewives of Jersey Shore.

Marital drift is a side-effect of two people all-in on raising kids and managing the American Dream. Time together typically has a business element to it. In the early stages of the drift, Kevin and Heidi thought they were doing fairly well managing the family.

HEIDI
Did you pay the electric bill?
KEVIN
Barely had enough. Did you see how high the visa bill was this month?
HEIDI
Oops! Sorry about that. Don't you remember I told you Stacy needed a new outfit for the skating event and Brandon's outgrown his hockey equipment?
KEVIN
Oh yeah. Kids are expensive.
HEIDI
By the way, don't make plans to play golf this weekend, the kids are in soccer tournaments.
KEVIN
Golf? Are you kidding me? I made plans to mow the lawn, seal the driveway, and power wash the siding.
HEIDI
Well, at least make an appearance at their games between your projects, Big Guy.
KEVIN
All right. Did I tell you my boss is flying into town on Monday, which means I'll be working more hours next week?
HEIDI
I better call my parents to see if they can help chauffeur the kids to their events. I can't leave the bank early, being manager. Were you able to fix the leak downstairs or should I call a plumber?
KEVIN
Leak fixed.
HEIDI
Good, 'cause now the dryer isn't drying.
KEVIN
I'm on it.
HEIDI
Way to go Mr. Fix-It, you sexy man.
KEVIN

I like where this is going.

Relationships can withstand the rigor of busy life for a stretch of time. However, when it becomes a pattern year after year, the drift expands and the relationship really suffers. Fast forward ten years into the marriage and the tone of the dialog between Kevin and Heidi becomes sharper.

KEVIN
What's with the attitude, Heidi? I walk in the door after a hard day's work and you greet me with a glare?
HEIDI
Where are your priorities? Work or family? I can't raise these kids on my own, Kevin. Brandon's behavior is out of control. He needs his father to step up.
KEVIN
Why would I want to do that when you step in and tell me how I'm doing it all wrong? No thanks.
HEIDI
Well, at least you could back me up and not take the kids' side in an argument.
KEVIN
What goes around comes around.
HEIDI
You know you could help more around the house. Lately, all you do is retreat to your man cave. I hate that gazebo!
KEVIN
I hate your shopping sprees! Why do you think I work the extra hours? You spend way beyond our means.
HEIDI
Want to talk about habits? It seems to me you're developing a habit of smoking pot again.
KEVIN
You'd smoke weed too if you had to put up with all the b*#@sh$@ I do at work and at home.
HEIDI

Oh, please. Give me a break. I bust my butt as much—if not more than you do.
KEVIN
I can't tell by looking at it.
HEIDI
Jerk. Don't bother looking for any tonight.
KEVIN
What else is new?

See how the respect dissipates with the drift? Tired couples fall prey to attacking each other. Disrespect sets the tone of many of their discussions, especially if they're in a drift. No longer allies, they become adversaries in a battle for respect. The problem is they are not getting or giving any respect. Criticism morphs into contempt and the relationship takes on an ugly tone. When marital drift extends too far, the relationship becomes toxic and needs intervention. Without it, the marriage is at risk of divorce. Marital counseling would be in order for the Hughes.

Bringing Respect Back In Civility

Couples who act uncivil toward each other need to be aware of how toxic it is for children. Incivility is one of the lower forms of human conduct. Children develop maladaptive ways of coping under this type of adult interaction. The toxic element may cause them to act out aggressively toward each other, their peers, or even adults. Some children display regressive behaviors, while others attempt to draw attention away by being perfect. Fundamentally, they all suffer from a lack of security caused by marital distress. Therefore, it behooves couples to stop engaging in conflict that has a contemptuous tone. Raise a white flag, call a truce, do whatever is necessary to stop the pattern of incivility in your interactions. I recommend couples seek counseling to learn how to manage conflict and speak respectfully toward each other.

The Conflict Cycle

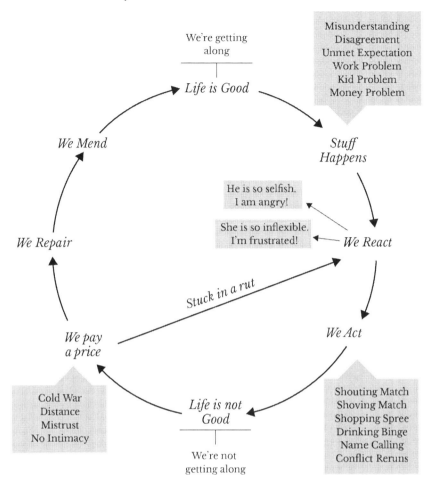

In my work with couples, I educate them on how a typical conflict cycle occurs. The model above illustrates a typical conflict cycle. We examine how their reactions intensify and perpetuate conflict, making it more unmanageable. I discuss how unresolved conflicts stockpiled around the relationship leave couples in a rut without a means to get out. Finally, I teach couples how to resolve and manage their conflicts so that their conflicts no longer dictate their relationship. This skill increases civility and respect in the marriage, while also giving the couple a sense of competence in working together as a team. Let me illustrate the cycle, assuming I am working with Kevin and Heidi.

COUNSELOR

So what would you two like to work on today?

HEIDI

Kevin is MIA when it comes to co-parenting, so I get the chore of keeping our two teenagers in line.

KEVIN

Yeah, if you mean "Mistakes In Action," because I never seem to parent to her expectations.

COUNSELOR

Okay, so you two don't seem to be on the same page on how to parent your kids.

HEIDI

Well, Kevin is way too harsh in his parenting approach and the kids don't listen to him.

KEVIN

How do you know? You always butt in and correct me in front of them. You're essentially telling them not to listen to me.

HEIDI

There are easier ways to get them to do what you want. Talking to them, listening to them, and meeting their needs gets results much easier than your approach.

KEVIN

I think she's too soft on our kids and they walk all over her. Just the other day, Brandon refused to get up for school. So what does Heidi do? She bribes him with twenty bucks.

HEIDI

I knew he needed the money for concert tickets. It worked didn't it? He did go to school.

KEVIN

Yeah, it worked. He got two for one. Twenty bucks in his pocket and a first row seat to watch you and me go another round of fighting.

COUNSELOR

Is this a typical pattern in your home?

HEIDI

Yeah. Pretty much.

COUNSELOR

Would you like to break this pattern?

KEVIN

Yeah, but I don't think it's possible.

COUNSELOR

Are you willing to give it a try?

KEVIN

That's what we're here for, I guess.

COUNSELOR

I'll walk you through a typical conflict cycle using the argument you had over Brandon. We'll trace the pattern and the outcome. Then I'll show you how and where to break the negative pattern so that you can increase your chance of a positive outcome.

KEVIN

Sounds good. It won't hurt to try. What we're doing now doesn't work.

COUNSELOR

Before the argument over Brandon, how were things between the two of you?

HEIDI

Things were fine.

KEVIN

Yeah, we were having a good morning.

COUNSELOR

So life was good?

KEVIN

Yep!

HEIDI

Agreed.

COUNSELOR

So that's the first stage of the conflict: life is good. Then, well, stuff happens. Brandon tested your limits.

KEVIN

He's good at that.

HEIDI

Brandon is a master of limit testing.

COUNSELOR

So now you're in the second stage: stuff happens. Something occurred that disrupted the day.

KEVIN

And how quickly it hit the fan!

COUNSELOR

Good observation, Kevin. Here's the third phase: we react. People react in two quick ways: thinking and feeling. For example, what were you thinking when you saw Heidi bribing Brandon to get up for school?

KEVIN

I was wondering why she lets him take advantage of her this way. He's not being respectful to his mother. He's using her.

COUNSELOR

How did you feel?

KEVIN

Angry at Brandon and Heidi. I also felt powerless because he doesn't listen to me and she won't let me do anything.

COUNSELOR

Heidi, what were you thinking at that moment in the conflict?

HEIDI

Honestly, I was so focused on getting Brandon up for school, I wasn't paying much attention to Kevin. I was hoping he would just leave me to do my job.

COUNSELOR

How did you feel at that moment?

HEIDI

I felt embarrassed that I had to stoop so low as to bribe Brandon to get up. I also felt angry at my son that he would humiliate me, but I didn't want him to know it.

COUNSELOR

Did you feel alone?

HEIDI

Yes! I didn't want to have to do this on my own. I was angry with Kevin that he was not helping, just criticizing my parenting.

COUNSELOR

Okay. We are now ready to examine the fourth phase: we act. These actions are based on your thoughts and feelings. Kevin, what did you do?

KEVIN

I told Heidi she was doing the wrong thing giving Brandon the money.

HEIDI

No, you yelled at me.

KEVIN

You're right. I yelled. I was so angry that he was winning and you were letting him.

COUNSELOR

Heidi, what did you do?

HEIDI

I yelled back at him and called him a jerk.

KEVIN

It got ugly from there. Let's see. We swore at each other. Criticized and blamed each other for Brandon's problems. Then we ignored each other the rest of the day. That sums up our typical pattern in a Brandon fight.

COUNSELOR

So now we are moving to phase five: life is not good.

HEIDI

No it wasn't. I left for work in tears. Found out later that Brandon cut class.

KEVIN

I was late to work because I missed the train.

COUNSELOR

Did you two make up before you left for work?

HEIDI

No. We were not in a making up mood.

KEVIN

Yeah, that rarely happens with us anymore.

COUNSELOR

Well, that takes us to phase six: we pay a price. These are the consequences that befall a marriage when a conflict is left unresolved.

KEVIN

We've got plenty of conflicts piled up.

COUNSELOR

Heidi, what does Kevin do to make you pay in a conflict?

HEIDI

That's easy, he retreats to his man cave and smokes weed.

COUNSELOR

Is that all?

HEIDI

Are you kidding? He also walks around pouting, criticizes me over little things, and doesn't lift a finger to help around the house.

COUNSELOR

Kevin, what does Heidi do to make you pay?

KEVIN

Pay is definitely the operative word. Heidi knows how spell revenge: V-I-S-A.

COUNSELOR

Is that all?

KEVIN

I would mention sex. But it's been so long since we've had any that I don't bother asking for it.

COUNSELOR

As you can see, you two are experts in getting revenge. The problem is, you are also experts in letting conflict own you. Your conflict resolution skills keep your marriage stuck in a rut.

HEIDI

That worries me. How do we get out of the rut?

COUNSELOR

Well, you don't seem to get to the seventh stage very often, if ever.

KEVIN

What stage is that?

COUNSELOR

I call it, "We repair." What I mean is you work together to repair the conflict.

KEVIN

How do we do that?

COUNSELOR

I'll make it easy for you to remember. Each step begins with the letter A. First step: Admit you are wrong for how you acted. Second step: Acknowledge how you hurt your partner. Third step: Accept responsibility for your actions. Fourth step: Ask for forgiveness. Fifth step: Agree to work on changing your attitude and/or behavior if it is a pattern in the relationship.

KEVIN

Easier said than done.

COUNSELOR

It does require some humility. However, your pride and defensiveness is what keeps you in a conflict mode.

HEIDI

That's true. We're so focused on winning an argument that we don't care what the outcome might be. Right now, we are not only hurting our marriage but we are also damaging our kids. We need to get back on track.

COUNSELOR

You need to get your respect back. Repairing together will help you get it back. Remember, it takes two to tango.

KEVIN

I admit yelling at Heidi doesn't fix the problem. It makes it worse.

HEIDI

It doesn't help that I handcuff you from parenting. I cannot criticize you for being an absentee parent if I push you away.

COUNSELOR

May I point out that this little dialog here was the two of you doing some repair work? How does it feel?

KEVIN

Weird, but good. I don't want Heidi to feel alone.

HEIDI

You don't? I thought you didn't care, Kevin. I feel sad that we have allowed our relationship to drift this far.

KEVIN

Maybe we can drift back.

COUNSELOR

This brings me to the eighth phase. I call it, "We heal." It takes time for a relationship to heal from conflict, no matter what size, shape, or degree of damage. Some conflicts heal within seconds. Others take minutes or hours. Then there are those that take days, weeks, and months.

HEIDI

So how do we heal?

COUNSELOR

One way is by bringing respect back. Agreeing to change your attitude and behavior has to be a mutual decision. Also, you need to give each other space to heal, grow and change. Patterns don't change overnight. You have to consciously work at them together.

KEVIN

I know I'm tired of fighting and feeling like I'm on the outside of the family.

HEIDI

I'm tired of going at it alone.

COUNSELOR

In the coming weeks, we can work together to change this pattern so that it works more evenly and efficiently in your marriage. In the meantime, I suggest you two give each other a high-five for working through the conflict cycle.

Breaking The Conflict Cycle

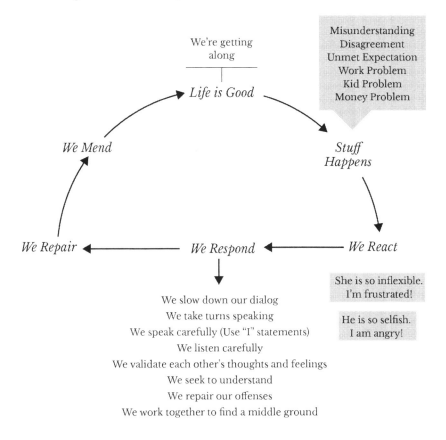

There are points of interruption in the conflict cycle that serve to avoid going from "life is good" to "life is not good." The key place to shift the pattern is in phase three: we react. Here, I train couples how to shift to a "we respond" mode of interaction illustrated in the model above. Reaction is quick, impulsive and autonomic. A response approach has a slower pace, using proficient communication skills. Here are four basic communication skills I teach my clients to use in responding to a conflict.

- I approach openly to engage you.
- I listen carefully to understand you.
- I respond empathically to validate you.
- I speak respectfully to convey myself to you.

Using this approach at the point of conflict reduces the risk of reactive behaviors and the negative consequences they deliver to the relationship.

One of the more challenging steps in the conflict cycle is "we repair". It involves taking ownership of offenses, acknowledging the hurt, and seeking forgiveness.[3] When asked what makes a happy marriage, Ruth Graham (the wife of Billy Graham) responded, "It is the merger of two forgivers." Repair addresses faults, not avoids them. Therefore, couples should not gloss over the repair phase. Note below the process I outline for couples. Each step is sequential and begins with the letter A for easy memorizing and recall. This process should be done honestly and humbly with the intent to repair the harm from the perspective the injured party. Your spouse/partner should get a sense that you understand how the offense hurt them.

Our Repair Kit

I **admit** my fault(s).

I **acknowledge** how my actions specifically hurt you.

I **accept** responsibility for my actions without blaming you.

I **ask** you to forgive me for my actions.

I **agree** to work on changing my behavior.

Changing patterns in relationships, like physical exercise, takes time, dedication, and practice. Initially, it's challenging because you come up against a resistance to change. However, after some work, you find the new pattern emerging more. Before long, you notice that you're managing conflict, rather than the other way around. With an increase in civility, you're ready for the next phase in bringing respect back to the marriage.

Bringing Respect Back In Friendship

When couples learn how to manage conflict, the outcome, as I have described, is civility. The truth is you fight less often and when you do, you find you are able to resolve it fairly. As this pattern of conflict management is established, it creates what marriage specialist[4] John Gottman calls "positive sentiment." Basically what this means is that the couple experiences a feeling of goodness and fondness in their relation-

---

3   Pentecostal Evangel, June 1, 1980, page 2

4   The Marriage Clinic - John Gottman, 1999 W.W. Norton & Company

ship. Rather than avoid each other, which is characteristic of couples who fight, companionship begins to emerge as a dynamic in the marriage. In other words, the couple enjoys spending time together.

Companionship is one of the underlying needs not being met in many marriages. Couples are not spending quality time together. Rather, the bulk of time and energy, as I stated earlier is invested in raising kids, managing a household, and working a job. Couples often report that they want to spend more time together but their schedules make it difficult, if not impossible. While this is a valid point, I find that people generally will make time for the things they enjoy.

The real issue with couples is not so much their busy schedules; it is the negative sentiment in the relationship that causes them to avoid spending time together. The excuse generally comes across in the question, "Why be together if all we are going to do is fight?" This is why I focus first on getting couples to bring civility back into their relationship by seeking to understand and validate each other.

Once couples are getting along, there is more incentive to spend time together. Suddenly, their tight schedules have more flexibility and they are able to make time for each other. Why? Because people make time for things they enjoy! Friendship allows couples to bring the old, good stuff back into the relationship as well as trying new things. Here's what I mean.

I notice that when couples get along, they also get back to things they once enjoyed doing together. For example, if they used to enjoy biking or dancing, they will tune up the bikes for a ride or go out for dinner and dancing. As for the new, many couples will explore things together they have never done before. The purpose is to get some fun and adventure back into the relationship. I know of couples who take art, dancing, or cooking classes together. Others have started hiking, traveling, biking.

To develop healthy friendship, you have to be willing to try things introduced by your partner. For example, my wife enjoys going to dressage competition, where horses prance in dance steps carefully choreographed by their riders. On the other hand, I enjoy going to the ball park to watch the Chicago White Sox. My wife is googylie-eyed when I sit next to her at a horse show. Likewise, I find nothing more exciting than munching on a couple of hotdogs, donning baseball caps, cheering and high-fiving my wife at a game. While we don't share each other's preferences, we encourage their existence in our relationship as a means of building companionship.

Friendship is more than doing fun things together. It is also getting along and having fun doing routine things. Common work responsibilities can be accomplished better by two people who like each other. Whether it is gardening, painting, or simple household chores, couples can experience a connection while getting the job done. My wife and I go to the local farmers market in our community on Saturdays during the summer. Almost every week, we run into a couple we both know through our professions. Over the course of time, we have become friends. What I like about this couple is the apparent companionship in their marriage. They have many challenges between managing a household, work, and having children with special needs. However, I am so impressed by their ability to handle the chronic stressors without attacking each other. They function so well as a team because they like each other and show respect.

Friendship is enhanced by remembering what you admire about your partner and expressing fondness. Couples in conflict are fixated on what they don't like about each other. Criticism and complaints generate much of the interaction. Couples in companionship focus on what they do like about their partners and express an appreciation for them. In fact, if you want to break the negativity cycle in your communication, try giving compliments and words of appreciation. However, don't assume it will improve things right away. You have to do it with some degree of regularity in order for the positive pattern to develop and your partner to reciprocate.

Bringing Respect Back In Intimacy

The prelude to intimacy is civility and friendship. Most couples cannot experience intimacy when they lack fondness and fight all the time. However, once you reach this level of respect, the relationship is ripe for intimacy. When I talk about intimacy with couples, I do not assume they are thinking the same thing. Generally speaking, men and women apply different meanings to the term. For men, intimacy is visual and related to sex. For women, it begins with an emotional connection initiated by talking or cuddling together. Actually, intimacy is both ends of the continuum and everything in-between. For example, couple intimacy can be experienced cooking a meal together, going for a walk, watching a movie, or sharing a private matter. Intimacy has a unique, personal meaning to every individual. Knowing this, it is important for couples to learn what intimacy means in the relationship so that they can strive together to meet each other's needs. Here are some starter questions to get the conversation going.

- What does intimacy mean to you?
- What do you think gets in the way of our intimacy?
- How can I be more of an intimate partner toward you?
- What do I do that hurts intimacy?
- What do I do that helps intimacy?

Intimacy intruders interfere with couples' need for romantic connection. The most common intruders are: busyness, children, arguments, and fatigue. In many dual-income households, couples leave one job and come home to another, running a household. A typical family calendar is event-filled, leaving very little room for unstructured time. At the end of the day, weary couples drag their bodies to bed, exhausted, desperately needing alone time to finally unwind. They may have a faint interest in sex, but don't have the energy it takes to fully engage with their partner. A marriage can withstand this on the short-term without it affecting intimacy. However, if a pattern of busyness develops, a martial drift is unavoidable and the level of intimacy will decrease over time.

Smart couples invest in their relationship by scheduling time together. Notice I said invest, not spend? Investing time in the marriage for companionship and intimacy will pay large dividends in the family as a whole. In my couples work, I operate off this premise: If you take good care of yourself, you will be a better partner for your marriage. If the two of you take good care of your marriage, you will be better parents for your kids. Let's take a closer look at how this works.

Emotional Tank Model

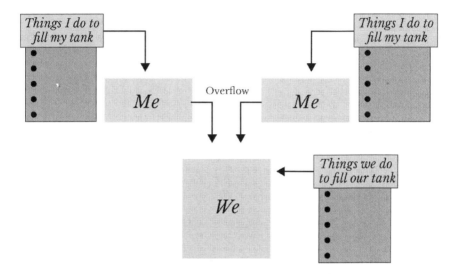

Taking care of yourself, as I discussed in chapter three, is paramount to healthy relationships. One key benefit illustrated in the diagram is that it fills your emotional tank. This is a critical component in emotional regulation. The more de-stressed you are, the less likely you will be reactive in your interactions with your spouse. Actually, you may find yourself being more responsive and caring toward her/him. Attitude and mood regulation are positively influenced by making regular deposits in your emotional tank.

A couple that values self-care will likely take a similar approach in the marriage. Again, this is a form of respect. It says, *Our marriage is important and we will do what it takes to invest in it*. If you notice in the model, couples can do a variety of things to invest in their relationship. If you want to fill the couple tank, I recommend you consider pockets of time and planned time to invest in the relationship. Pockets of time are simply the moments during the day when you can connect as a couple. It could be a cup of coffee in the morning, a glass of wine at night, or going for a walk around the block. As for planned time, I offer the following formula to couples: weekly date nights, quarterly overnights or weekends away, and biannual vacations without the children. Vacations are not recommended when the children are really young, but overnights and weekends may work. The point is you have to be intentional about making time for your relationship and it will require that you establish a pattern to make it happen.

On date nights, I encourage couples to set boundaries to limit talk about family and work issues and invest the time in reconnecting dialog, talking about each other. My wife and I make it a practice on date nights to talk about books we're reading, interests we are involved in, or issues of the day. We also enjoy connecting on spiritual matters. Discussion about work and/or family matters is limited to about fifteen minutes of de-stressing conversation where we can listen, support, or solve a problem.

You may find it difficult to know what to talk about when the routine issues are not on the agenda, but with some practice, you may engage in some interesting conversations. We should never lose our curiosity about our partners. There is always something to learn or a story to hear that you haven't heard before. Also, there are also those stories that you enjoy hearing again, because they are deeply meaningful and they connect you intimately.

Bringing Intimacy Back After a Deep Marital Wound

The process of bringing intimacy back can be relatively easy or complex, depending on the couple. For couples who have experienced a drift in their relationship but have a moderate degree of respect, getting intimacy back may not be too complicated. Perhaps a dialog around the questions above can be a starting point. Making deposits in the relational tank won't hurt either.

For couples embroiled in conflict or who have experienced a breach of trust caused by infidelity for example, the process of repairing intimacy is more delicate. Let's take the Hughes for example. When Heidi hit the breaking point, she did not hold back, but told Kevin how she really felt in the marriage. He unloaded his negative sentiment toward her as well. The exchange wasn't pleasant. His suspicions about her infidelity came up.

KEVIN

Who is Tom?

HEIDI

I don't know who you are talking about. We know several people named Tom.

KEVIN

Don't play dumb with me, Heidi. I read a text message.

HEIDI

He's a guy who used to be in my Pilates class. No big deal. He is just an acquaintance.

KEVIN

Really? The text had a flirtatious tone. He asked if your shoulders were still sore. What's going on here?

HEIDI

(Barely holding it together)

You want to know the truth, Kevin? I'll tell you what's going on. I have been so lonely in this marriage for such a long time. Whenever I reached out to you, you were enveloped in smoke. Oh, how I *hate* that gazebo! I have been hurting for such a long time. Stupid me, I crossed the line. I had sex with Tom. Talk about going from bad to worse. That was the biggest mistake in my life. Go ahead and unleash your anger, Kevin.

Heidi's affair, much like Kevin's substance abuse, is a symptom of a toxic marriage. It indicates a major drift, leaving the relationship loveless and dispassionate. Polarized in their positions and self-protective, this couple operates in a defensive-reactive mode, with neither willing to risk vulnerability. Sadly, they cannot work toward intimacy on their own. Repairing wounds and rebuilding trust on both sides is necessary before intimacy can be restored. This was the breaking point that drove the Hughes to marital counseling.

If your relationship mirrors the Hughes in some way, in the sense that you have drifted apart and walls of resentment are building, I suggest you consider counseling as a means of beginning the process of repairing the relationship and bringing respect back. Attempting to repair on your own, as you probably know by now, is difficult because of the reactive nature of the relationship. Working with a professional who is skilled in marital or relational therapy is helpful because a counselor's position of neutrality can serve to disarm the tension and move you from an adversarial position to allies working together against the problems in your marriage. In the end, a respectful relationship repairs hurts, restores trust, establishes security, and enhances friendship and intimacy.

When I work with couples, I inform them that I look at their feet to determine if they stand a chance to succeed in counseling. After they look down at their feet with confused expressions, I clarify that I mean figuratively, not literally. You see, what I want to know is if they have one or both feet in to work on their relationship. This is an important assessment that will guide my efforts going forward.

By the end of the first session, I have a fairly good idea of where their feet are in the marriage and I let them know.

I may say, "Mrs. Jones, by listening carefully to you for the past hour, I would have to say that you have one foot in the marriage and one foot out, but in the past, both feet were in. Mr. Jones, for years you had no feet in while Mrs. Jones begged you to come into counseling. However, you would have none of that psycho-babble nonsense and dismissed her time and again, causing walls of resentment to build in her heart. Now Sir, you have both feet in all the way. Unfortunately, you waited too long and Mrs. Jones is tired and is convinced she is better served living without you. Fortunately for you, she is giving this marriage one last chance. Somehow, you have to convince her by what you do over the course of our time together that it's safe for her to move her other foot back into the marriage."

Bringing respect back to your marriage is possible no matter what condition you are in, if you both have both feet in the relationship. I have worked with couples in all degrees of distress from a minor drift to major damage. When both feet are in, the couples generally succeed in repairing their marriage. Unfortunately, some do not and the relationship ends. There are also the unforeseen cases when the couple who are on the brink of divorce, put both feet into counseling, roll up their sleeves to work, and in the end have a better marriage than they imagined.

This is true even in marriages injured by infidelity.[5] In their book,

---

5   Getting Past the Affair - Snyder, Baucom & Coop-Gordon, 2007, The Guilford Press

"Getting Past the Affair: A Program to Help You Cope, Heal, and Move On—Together or Apart", authors Douglas Snyder, Donald Duncan, and Kristina Coop Gordon report that seventy percent of couples survive infidelity and close to fifty percent achieve a level of intimacy that exceeds what they experienced before the affair. I have found this to be the case with several of the couples I have worked with in couples counseling. In these situations, we leveled the old marriage and, with a collaborative effort, constructed a new one. The transformative process in these relationships is amazing to observe.

Where To Start Bringing Respect Back

Where do you need to focus to bring respect back in your marriage? In rules of engagement, do you act civilly toward each other? Or, do you find yourselves constantly embroiled in nasty conflicts that rarely are resolved? Do you use hurtful language or belittle your partner in an argument? If so, the starting place for you is bringing respect back in how you interact. You need to think about your behavior and its affect on your partner. Furthermore, you have to learn how to manage your emotions and behaviors in a manner that conveys respect even though you may disagree with your spouse's point of view.

If civility is not a serious problem, how does the friendship factor function in your marriage? Are you too busy to have fun together? Too exhausted to play? Perhaps the remedy in your relationship is some scheduled play time together. By the way, don't forget to include some time for yourself. You're not going to be the best for your partner if you are not de-stressing and depositing into your emotional tank. Use the Emotional Tank Model to begin work on this important investment in yourself and your marriage.

Finally, how is the intimacy working in your marriage? Do you know what the term means to your partner? Have you adequately conveyed what intimacy means to you? If you're not sure what it means, it is probably good that you spend some time becoming more informed on what intimacy means in your marriage. You might be surprised! Use the brief intimacy questionnaire in this chapter, sit down with a cup of

Java and have a conversation with your mate to craft a mutually satisfying, working definition of intimacy in your marriage. Make a pledge to work together to rekindle or enhance the flames of intimacy in your relationship. In the area of sexual intimacy, if you are experiencing intimacy intruders such as erectile dysfunction, premature ejaculation, or female sexual arousal disorder, I recommend you seek professional help to address these conditions.

What is most important right now is that you do something to bring respect back into your marriage. If you wait for your spouse to act, you will likely remain in the dance of disrespect. Remember what I said about the dance? Someone has to initiate. Perhaps you can change the dance routine at home. Invite your spouse out for a walk, a cup of coffee, or do something you know they would enjoy to get their attention. Begin a safe dialog about wanting to connect more, have fun and get along better. Be creative!

Some of you may read this and feel anger surge in your heart. You have been the initiator and your partner has not responded to your cues. In your case, it might be good to stop initiating. I certainly do not want to suggest something to you that will set you up for more rejection. You are in a state of vulnerability in your marriage where the drift places your marriage at risk. I suggest you find someone to talk to who can offer support and guidance through this difficult time.

If you are the spouse of the partner I just described, you have work to do and do it fast. You have to become the initiator in your marriage to begin the process of bringing respect back. No excuses, just actions. What will be your next move? Do you know how serious the problem in your marriage is from your partner's perspective? You might be surprised to find out! Kevin Hughes had no clue how bad things were in his marriage. He was escaping into his cave. Escaping is no longer acceptable. Engaging your spouse is your next move.

So what are you going to do next?

Chapter Five

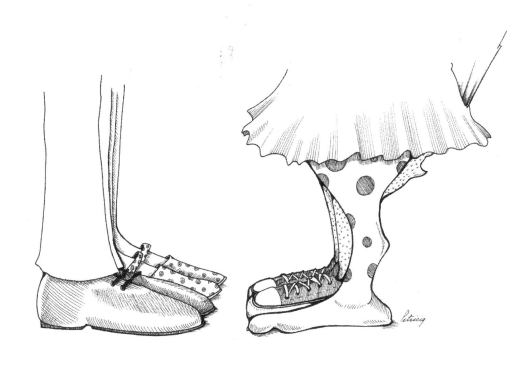

Bringing Respect Back Into The Family

"I know you took it and I want it back right now!"

Stacy's fierce expression is fixed on Brandon's dismissing glance.

"I have no idea what you're talking about, Drama Queen, but you are interrupting my game, so go away before I make you."

The sibs have engaged in a dance they do nearly every day with flawless execution. It is an adolescent dance of disrespect. Now its Stacy's move. "Look, I'll tear your room apart if you don't hand my over my iPod. Just because you broke yours in one of your fits of rage doesn't give you a right to take mine!"

Brandon moves in perfect synchrony with his sister. "The hell you will. Step one foot in my room and I will break it. You have no proof I stole your iPod. Besides, I hate your freaking music."

Fearless of her brother's threat, Stacy intensifies the dance. "Too late, you fool. I already confiscated your weed. Either you give me back my property or I hand yours over to mom!"

Brandon blasts into his room to locate his stash, only to find that Stacy has already made her move. Furious, he punches a hole in his bedroom wall—not the first time—and rushes back to the dance floor where Stacy is ready to stand toe-to-toe in the next dance movement.

"I'm not afraid of your threats, Brandon! You hit me and I'll call the police and I will also give them your weed."

"I hate you, Drama Queen" Brandon snaps, as he reaches into the pocket of his cargo shorts and pulls out Stacy's iPod. "Hand over my stuff and you can have this back. Besides, I just borrowed it. You didn't have to get your panties in a wad." Now in the final stage of the dance, the two step away from each other, exchange glares and possessions, knowing that while this battle is over, the sibling war rages on.

Quite intense exchange huh? I wish I could say that I was embellishing here, but quite honestly, this scenario resembles sibling relationships in many households. Not all reach the level of intensity depicted in the exchange between Brandon and Stacy, but an attitude of disrespect permeates many sibling relationships today. This is not a new phenomenon; truth be told, sibling rivalry existed since the dawn of time. The Biblical story of the first family described how Cain's jealousy of Abel got the best of him and he murdered his brother.[6] The Book of Proverbs says, *"A friend loves at all times, but a sibling is born for adversity."*

Think about your childhood. Was it like *Leave It To Beaver*? Or was it more like a reality TV show? I remember in my family, being the fourth born of five kids, I had conflicts with my siblings. It's just a part of growing up. I'm sure you have your stories too, unless you were an only child. So what's the big deal? If it is a given that sibling conflict is a norm, then why address it here?

In my work with families and through general observation, the level of disrespect among kids in this generation cuts deeper than in the past. In fact, in some households siblings have a general dislike for each other and find pleasure in getting one another in trouble. They compete not only for parental attention, but for ranking and control within the family. Typically, the primary form of interaction is annoying behavior. They prefer pushing each other's buttons over getting along. This is how Brandon and Stacy acted toward each other. Everything about their relationship was separate: friends, interests, music, styles, and they preferred it this way. They did not hang out together nor engage in conversation. At their best, they coexisted while at their worst they fought like mortal enemies. They did nothing to invest in a close sibling relationship.

Families Upside Down

One of my big concerns is how the family is being restructured

---

6   The Holy Bible, Book of Proverbs 17:17

in our culture. When I was growing up, children feared disappointing their parents. Today, parents fear their children disliking them! The traditional, hierarchical model, with parents holding a position of authority and children below has been inverted. In many households, children have equal status with parents and in some cases hold more power than the adults. Have you noticed lately how kids talk to their parents? Hardly a hint of respect: they use words in a cutting manner that suggests they, not their parents, are controlling the relationship.

Working with kids and teens in counseling, I often ask them how they define a parent. Some of the responses fit the general definition, while many are quite disturbing. There is a growing sentiment among young people today that parents exist for the sole purpose of serving kids, period. Another alarming element is that this generation holds no obligation to reciprocate anything toward their parents. From their point of view, parents are on call to take care of them. Having a sense of entitlement, they view themselves as kings and queens of the family who expect to receive without obligation to give. When parents expect kids to clean their room or do some basic household chore, they are ignored. It may take several attempts to get compliance: asking, threatening, bribery, but there is no guarantee the task will get done—at least by the kids. Unfortunately, in some households the children have trained their parents to do their job, whether it be chores, cleaning their rooms, or doing their homework! How do they do this? Kids play on two primary emotional triggers: guilt and fear.

Parents fall prey to their kids' tactics when an undercurrent of fear or guilt influences parenting. Many parents overburdened by work schedules and household duties feel guilty not spending enough time with their kids. Parental responsibilities are often delegated to daycare workers, nannies, or grandparents. A lack of a secure bond, combined with a busy schedule, creates tension in parent-child relationships. Consequently, unconfident parents use pragmatic solutions to get compliance from their children. Bribery and indulgence are two primary tools parents use to get their children to behave. Constantly appeasing children's gratification impulses is dangerous to their development, not to mention the parent-child relationship. Knowing how to get what they want, kids will constantly divert parents' attention toward them in calculated measures to get their wants met. Notice I said "wants" not "needs".

In the previous chapter we observed how Brandon was able to extract money for concert tickets from his mother's purse without stealing it. He simply stalled getting up for school until bribery was offered by Heidi. Brandon got the money, she got him up out of bed. On other occasions he procrastinated doing his homework knowing it would force her to take action. When threats and bribes didn't work, she did the homework for him. Alas, here is an example of how guilt drives a parenting approach. Heidi cannot bear to see her kids fail. What will it mean for their future? How will that reflect on her role as a parent?

Most parents rate their success by the success of their children growing up. This occurs in all phases of life, including transition into adulthood. Problems occur when parents over-focus on their children's behavior in academics and activities such as sports, music or dancing. Kids feel the pressure from parents to succeed and will often take one of two approaches. They may compete hard to succeed and gain the approval of their parents, or they may resist the pressure and not perform up to expectations.

Either way, kids under this kind of pressure often believe (rightly or wrongly) their worth in the eyes of their parents is linked to their performance. They don't feel valued apart from what they do, nor do they feel accepted for who they are. Consequently, an underlying resentment forms that places a wedge in the parent-child relationship, often leading children to pull away from their parents or act out to get revenge. Experts agree it is essential for parents to instill in their children an understanding that they are loved and accepted unconditionally. I will develop this approach in the following chapter.

A performance dynamic may also cause problems among siblings because it establishes a competitive element that alters the tone of their relationship. Vying for parental approval, siblings may compete with each other as rivals for attention and adulation. While some rivalry is normal, it can become toxic if parents put too much emphasis on performance.

In the Hughes household, Brandon was aversive toward success and got attention by doing the opposite of what his parents wanted. Stacy on the other hand, performed well in school, excelled in extracurricular activities, and obeyed the rules when it mattered. The more Stacy shined, the more Brandon acted out and vise-versa. Every disappointing look from his parents confirmed Brandon's mistaken belief that they didn't love him, certainly not as much as Stacy. While every approving gesture confirmed Stacy's belief that she outranked her brother because she believed her parents loved her more. Unfortunately, this dynamic prevented Brandon and Stacy from forming a healthy bond, one that would foster a positive sentiment toward each other. Instead, they were adversaries competing for parental attention and hated each other.

Bringing respect back into a family is one of the biggest cries I hear in my work with families. Parents are distraught over the blatant lack of respect in their homes. They work so hard to provide a house with all the amenities they think will make them happy, yet everyone is miserable when together. The haven of rest functions more like a war zone where individuals retreat to their rooms following daily battles in the family. Teenagers also want respect from their parents, and they are less likely to give respect until they get it first. Let's take a look at the dance movements that help bring respect back in the family.

First Move: Parents Model Respect With Each Other

You cannot expect someone to give what you don't give yourself. You want your kids to respect you? You want them to respect each other? Then the place to start is with yourself. You may wonder why I focus on you. After all, our parents didn't make it a priority to model respect; they simply demanded it from us. "I'm your parent. Show some respect!" No questions asked. Respect was what kids must show parents, not the other way around. It was a matter of rank.

Here, we have identified part of the problem. Our parents were not exactly good models of respect. They were tough authority figures who imposed their wills on us. This was particularly true of fathers. They were hardworking individuals who didn't have much tolerance for disorder in the home. Nor did they have much patience with training and modeling respect in their interactions with children. Mothers were expected to do the training. Modeling was more likely to come from mothers than fathers. However, with the mounting pressures of dual roles and responsibilities as women entered the workforce, parental involvement in the raising of children was diminished. This presented challenges in family bonding, structure, and raising children.

Due to existing family structures characterized by busy schedules and less quality contact, it is even more essential that respect be the guiding force in relationships. Establishing respect lies squarely on the shoulders of parents. It is also important to remember that humans are social learners. Behaviors are more caught that taught. Actions speak louder than words. True, your kids learn more from what you do than what you say. Consider this quote from Ralph Waldo Emerson: "Who you are speaks so loudly, I can't hear what you are saying." Kids can't hear, "Show some respect" if they can't see it modeled in our actions first.

No doubt, it is hard to be respectful when you are stressed out most of the time. Think about it. How often are your interactions with your kids done while multitasking? You pick up the kids from school and have to rush them to soccer practice, or a doctor's appointment, while you are on the phone attending to a work related matter. Don't forget that you have dinner to figure out, kids' homework, the laundry, bills to pay, and the pile of unfinished work you had to bring home. What you don't need is kids piling on your heavy load by acting unruly. It is easy for a parent to lose patience and yell at their kids. The impatience combined with yelling is an uncontrolled reaction that conveys disrespect.

Now think about the most common problem parents see in their children. Most often it is displayed in a lack of patience with each other, rudeness or your basic button-pushing behavior. Before long, the parent is baited into the fray as an adjudicator of the conflict. In a matter of minutes, bedlam breaks out. Parents yell at their children, children yell at each other, and parents and children yell back and forth. Crazy, huh? Out of control? A typical day in your family? It is in many families. They are doing a dance of disrespect and cannot stop until one or more gets their feelings hurt. A daily habituation of this dance turns companions into combatants. This is not what families want, but they cannot seem to break the pattern. The solution is learning the dance of respect. It starts with someone in the household setting a different tone of interaction, a tone of respect.

Commanding respect and demanding respect are two different things. Demanding respect is conveyed by words and threats. This was the paradigm our parents followed. Commanding respect is an influential process that happens when one interacts with another in a consistently respectful manner. Let's examine how this would look in the Hughes household if the parents decided to set the tone.

The first change we would notice is in how the parents interact with each other. Kevin would work on changing some of his negative patterns. Rather than criticize Heidi about her parenting skills, he would compliment her regularly. This would indicate a shift of focus from negative to positive.

Second, Kevin would move from the outside of the family circle to the inside by being more involved overall. Kevin might begin by trying to understand where Heidi is coming from on the issues of parenting. If he listens well and conveys an understanding of what Heidi is trying to communicate, it will show her respect and likely shift them from adversaries to allies in parenting.

Layers of respect can be added as Kevin asks Heidi how he can be more helpful to her in parenting their children. With ideas from Heidi, Kevin can come alongside her as a partner in parenting. This moves Kevin from the outside of the circle of parenting to the inside. To support Kevin's active parenting, Heidi will have to avoid criticizing his efforts if they don't align with how she does things. Respectful dialog, combining affirmation of effort and suggestions, will be a better approach.

Working as a team, the couple is able to present a united front to the children, shifting the power balance back to the parental hierarchy. Likewise, Heidi can show Kevin respect by focusing on the positive and soliciting ideas from him on how to handle tough situations, for example, Brandon's power play. The reciprocity of respectful dialog, understanding, validation, and accommodation enhances respect and further substantiates the parents' position of authority in the home.

Second Move: Parents Show Respect To Their Kids

The second movement is showing respect toward the children. Being on the inside of the family circle also means that Kevin has to earn the respect of his children. Being more active in establishing and enforcing the rules won't endear Kevin to his kids. Respect will not be given based on his power to control, but on his power to love unconditionally. Remember: Actions speak louder than words. Kevin will need to start building a relationship with his kids on a one-to-one basis. On some level, he will need to enter their world to discover who they are. For Kevin, it won't be easy. He lost the respect of his kids years ago, so they won't come around easily.

Parents like Kevin should expect strong resistance from their kids. He will be tested and retested before he can earn their respect. For example, let's look at his relationship with Brandon. Kevin might begin by playing some video games with Brandon or watching a movie of his choice with him. Hanging out with his son sends the message that he matters for who he is, not what he does. If Kevin can withstand the resistance of his son, communication will open and Brandon will eventually enjoy hanging with his dad, though he may not admit it.

Over time, as consistency establishes a respectful pattern of interaction, the father and son bond will strengthen, which gives Kevin the ability to influence positive change in his son. When it comes time to set a limit, Brandon may be more likely to comply out of his growing respect of his father. By observing Kevin's controlled demeanor in a conflict situation, Brandon may likely dial down how he responds to his parents, or his sister for that matter. Perhaps having more time with his kids and less time in his cave will motivate Kevin to conquer some of his negative habits, such as smoking marijuana. This may also open up dialog with his son about his habit.

Showing respect to your kids is based on your ability to control how you interact with them. As I stated earlier, kids will push your buttons. If you react to them, you are likely to lose control. If you respond to them, you will probably maintain control. Acting in a respectful manner requires control of your emotions and behavior. Emotional regulation is a key to respectful interactions. If you are angry, it is important that you express it in a controlled manner that conveys your point without amping up the problem. Shouting, hitting, or threatening behavior is a sign that your anger is too hot and behavior disrespectful. You can expect a negative reaction from your kids that will only make the matter worse.

Third Move: Parents Set The Respect Bar For The Family

The third movement in creating a respectful dance is setting a bar of respect for family interactions. This involves training and holding your kids accountable for how they act toward the other members of the family. This shift will be easier once you have set the bar by modeling respect. When you set and hold a tone of respect, others will generally rise to your level. It is the law of reciprocity in motion. Remember, behavior is better caught than taught.

Once you have set the bar of respect in your marriage and how you function as parents, you are ready to establish expectations for your kids. This will be easier once you are on the same page and function as a team. By combining your individual strengths in parenting, you will be able to collaborate on the expectations you have for a respectful family. These will become rules of engagement you can teach and train your kids to follow.

Implementing rules of engagement in your family will take time and require consistent effort and patience. Teaching is being clear on what your expectations are for the family. Training combines modeling and shaping this behavior in your children. I'll simplify the process by introducing you to the two-step, one-step dance for parents to do with their children.

Doing the Two-Step Dance

Training involves a two-step dance for parents and a one-step dance for kids. The two-step is simple to remember: *step in* and *step back*. For the kids, the one-step is *step up*. Not too difficult to remember, is it? Let's take a closer look at the parents' routine first.

In the training phase, stepping in begins with teaching kids what respect looks like. For example, if you are having a conversation with a child or teenager and they start talking over you, this becomes a time to teach them how a respectful conversation flows. In a teaching moment, a parent might communicate the following to the child.

"I can see you want to get your point across because you are talking over me. If we keep doing this, it will go nowhere and we will both be frustrated. Allow me to finish my point by listening without interrupting. I promise to keep it short. Afterwards, you can make your point and I will offer you the same courtesy of listening and perhaps we can resolve the matter in shorter time."

Notice how the parent remains calm, does not snap at the child, and explains how a more respectful approach works. This moment of stepping in to teach is likely to shift the dance in the right direction.

The next move, step back, is necessary for the child to do their move, step up. The step-back is a hard move for some parents because it requires restraint and patience. A tendency exists for some parents to step in too soon to correct a behavior. Impatient parents react to their children and quickly resort to criticism to get their point across. Unfortunately, this does not motivate kids to step up. Changing behavior is a process that happens over time. It requires a coaching approach that instructs proper behavior and instills confidence.

Let's see how this would work in the Hughes household. Kevin and Heidi have been doing a much better job of showing respect to each other and working as a team in parenting their two teenagers. They've noticed how rude Brandon and Stacy can be toward each other, so they target this as a behavior they want the teens to work on. Over dinner, they raise the concern with Brandon and Stacy about the pattern of rudeness in their relationship and inform them that they want them to work on being more respectful. When the request is made, notice how the two adversaries immediately form an alliance of resistance against the parents.

BRANDON
What do you mean we're rude?
STACY
Yeah. This is just how teenagers talk to each other today. You just have to get used to it.
KEVIN
Well, they may act that way outside, but inside this home, we expect you to show some respect.
BRANDON
So you expect us to pretend we like each other and be polite. It's not going to happen.
STACY

Nice try Dad, but we are not going to be the Brady Bunch. Welcome to the real world.

HEIDI

You don't have to like what we are asking you to do, but we expect you to work at it.

BRANDON

What's the purpose here? I don't get it. All of a sudden you two start acting all nice and you expect us to march in line with you? Not happening. It was your constant fighting that started all this crap in the first place. Now all of a sudden you're changing the rules? Sorry, but it's a little too late for that.

KEVIN

I get your point, Brandon. You two grew up listening to your mother and I fight all the time. We didn't do a good job of showing respect to each other. Unfortunately, you were caught in the crossfire of our arguments. We're sorry for putting you through this. But as you can probably see, we have realized some things and are changing our ways with each other and you kids. We want you to change with us. Your mom and I are working hard at not being rude toward each other and as your parents we are establishing new rules of engagement for all of us. If we can change, we are confident you and Stacy can be nicer toward each other.

STACY

It really scared me when you and mom fought all the time. After a while I went into my shell. I stopped caring for anyone except me. I'm afraid this change won't last and things will go back to the way they were.

HEIDI

I hear you, Stacy. I guess on some level we feel the same. But we're working hard on our relationship and we like where we are now. I don't think your father and I want to go back there either. I also know what it is like to go into a shell, Stacy. There is a risk coming out of it. So I understand if you are a little apprehensive.

BRANDON

So, what is it exactly we are supposed to do?

KEVIN

Good question Brandon. It's fairly simple. We want you to stop some things and start some things. Here are the things we want you to stop. First of all, stop saying mean things to each other and using four-letter words for emphasis. No rude comments on how one looks or dresses. No taking personal property without permission. No put-downs or innuendos. Now, for the things we want you to start. Be complimentary. Say "please" and "thank you" when you need something. Try to listen better. That's it for starters. Let's see how you do.

BRANDON
So what happens if we don't do it?
KEVIN
Well, then you restrict yourself I guess.
BRANDON
What do you mean by that?
KEVIN
If you choose not to respect others then you set the terms for exchange. So later in the day when you ask for the keys to the car, I will have to decline to give you the privilege of the car because you declined to show people respect. In this case, you restricted yourself from use of the car because you chose not to follow the family policy on respect. However, tomorrow is a new day. You can try to work on showing respect and if successful will be given the privilege of driving the car.
BRANDON
Whatever.

Notice how the parents respond to the resistance of their teenagers. They do not react, nor engage in a power struggle. Rather, they listen carefully, validate their kids' concerns, repair the hurt, and offer reassurance that they are on a new path. They understand that the resistance of their kids is not rooted in teenage rebellion. Rather, it is a self-protective strategy used to cope in the negative family environment they lived in most of their lives.

Having this perspective enables the parents to be firm in their expectations, yet patient with their kids while they learn to shift their behavior. Kevin stepped in to answer Brandon's question on what they were supposed to do, by instructing him on what behaviors he and his sister were to stop doing and what behaviors they were to start doing. It is important for parents to be clear with their kids on the expectations and what specific behavior(s) they want them to work on.

Keep in mind, you don't want to overwhelm your kids with a list of things to work on. Target one or two behaviors at most. The Hughes targeted rudeness as a behavior to eliminate and respect as a behavior to develop. After he informed Brandon of the new policy, Kevin stepped back and waited for Brandon to respond. Brandon tested his father further by questioning what would happen should he not comply with the rules. Kevin stepped in again to inform his son of the consequences of breaking the rules. However, he framed it not as a punishment, but rather as an outcome of self-restriction on Brandon's part. The use of language here is important in gaining compliance. Certain words, such as punishment, or consequences are triggers for resistance with many teens today. The use of these terms may have the opposite effect on motivation. By choosing his words carefully, Kevin was able to answer the question without being baited into a power struggle. This tactic punctuated his authority as the parent.

The next step here is for these parents to "step back" in order to give their teens the opportunity to "step up" and demonstrate that they can "work out" the rudeness and "work in" the respect. Because these are ingrained patterns of interaction, it will take time for change to occur. Parents have to understand this and exercise patience with their kids. Stepping in too frequently to point out mistakes will be counterproductive to the goal of shaping new behavior. For Kevin and Heidi, this meant working as a team, not allowing the kids to play one parent against the other, and keeping their own attitudes in check. Let's see how they did the two-step dance with their teens. The conversation begins with breakfast.

KEVIN
So, what are your plans today?
BRANDON
Skip school, hang at the mall, and invite some friends over tonight for some pizza and Xbox.
KEVIN
I like how you have your day planned out. However, I don't think Xbox will happen if the other two plans you've made do.

BRANDON
No seriously, I'm inviting friends over tonight after school, so can you order some pizza, Mom?
HEIDI
I haven't thought about dinner plans yet. It might be doable. What do you think, Kevin?
KEVIN
Possible. Let's see how Brandon does working out the rudeness and working in the respect today. He's doing much better with us, but I'd like to see him step it up with Stacy.
BRANDON
What about her? She is rude to me all the time.
KEVIN
(With a smile)
Nice try! But we are here talking to you about you showing some respect. You cannot control your sister, but you can control yourself.
HEIDI
We can see you are working at it, Brandon. When Stacy pushes your buttons, what do you think you can do?
BRANDON
I try walking away, but it's hard. She likes getting the last word in. Like she's on some power trip.
KEVIN
Perhaps you both like having the last word. It is like that with mom and I sometimes and it usually doesn't end well. So we work at not pushing each other's buttons.
Stacy enters the kitchen.
STACY
No one talk to me, I'm in a bad mood.
HEIDI
Thanks for the heads up.
BRANDON
What else is new, Drama Queen?
STACY
Shut up, Brandon! Why don't you go away?

BRANDON
Not a bad idea. Besides, if I don't leave now I'll be late for the mall. Err, I mean school.
KEVIN
I noticed some button pushing with your sister. I suggest you pay more attention to how you talk to Stacy if you want to see a pizza delivery tonight.
BRANDON
Point made. Working on it.
Brandon retreats upstairs, grabs his backpack and heads back to the kitchen to grab coke from the fridge.
BRANDON
Want some orange juice, Stacy?
STACY:
(Surprised)
Huh?
BRANDON:
(Handing her a glass of orange juice)
Sorry about the drama queen comment.
STACY
Thanks for the juice.

The Dance Of Respect In Action

There are several family dynamic shifts observable in this breakfast scenario. The first noticeable shift is the power in the family returning to the parents. Brandon may have set his agenda for the day, but it now had to go through the approval of his parents and it was based on his compliance with the family policy about showing respect. The parents worked as a team throughout the interaction with Brandon and kept the boundaries firm. They also used positive words and instilled confidence in him, noting areas of improvement while continuing to shape the behavior with his sister. No evidence of a power struggle is seen in this interaction.

This also suggests a shift in Brandon's relationship with his parents. He is starting to show more respect toward them. He is stepping up in how he interacts with his parents. When Brandon makes a rude comment to his sister, the parents did not criticize him. Instead, Kevin stepped in to dialog with Brandon about where his behavior is taking him in reference to his goal (pizza night with friends) and advised him to work on turning it around. Kevin's newfound influence is evident in Brandon's decision to repair his rude comment by offering Stacy an orange juice with his apology.

A test for the parents would be a scenario in which Brandon did not turn his behavior around and exhibited rude behavior for the rest of the day. Here, the parents would have to enforce the terms of the policy and not allow Brandon to have friends over for pizza and Xbox. They could inform him that tomorrow is a new day and discuss with him what he might do differently, if he is open for discussion. If he is angry, they have to remain firm in their decision and remind themselves that he will get over it. If they give in because they don't want to deal with his anger, then they are essentially relinquishing power to their son and their efforts to teach him to be respectful are thwarted.

Summarizing the Two-Step, One-Step Approach

Let me summarize how the two-step dance approach functions in parenting. Stepping in is essentially about teaching and shaping behavior. Stepping back is about observing and waiting. Parents step in to teach kids what they need to know to manage themselves. They step back to observe how the kids are doing stepping up to attempt the behavior. They step in again to correct or shape the behavior by enforcing consequences (natural and logical) and talking with the child or teen about what will help them succeed. Then they step back again to allow the child or teen to continue to master the behavior.

Stepping back, the waiting part, clarifies the boundaries about who is responsible for the behavior, the child or the parent. If the parent is stepping in too soon or too often, it confuses the child, lowers their confidence and sets the stage for a power struggle. Children who think their parents do not have confidence in them will act in ways to reinforce this belief, thus forming a negative pattern of an over-functioning parent and under-functioning child.

Doing the One-Step Dance

As important as it is for parents to learn how to do the two-step dance, it is also essential that children embrace the one-step response. Their task is to step up and do the behavior expected of them. In the case of the Hughes family, Brandon and Stacy had to step up by replacing rudeness with respect. When rudeness was shown, their parents stepped in with consequences, or as Kevin framed it to Brandon: "You're restricting yourself." Conversely, when they acted respectfully, the outcome was positive.

Without reciprocity, family respect doesn't come full-circle. It is easier to instill a value of respect in the family when children are young and more responsive to parental influence. The challenge many families face today is instilling a respectful attitude where disrespect has been the norm. Getting teens to step up and be responsible is no easy task. Our culture of entitlement does not support the step-up measure. It promotes a self-focused mindset that impairs an individual's ability to think about the needs of others. People are often viewed as objects that perform certain duties to satisfy the wants of the child or adolescent.

How does this translate into family life? It appears we have spawned a generation of young people who want parents to satisfy their needs without an obligation to reciprocate. Stepping up to perform a task, behavior, or role is intrusive and intimidating to a self-focused individual. The underlying thought process might be, *Don't ask me to do anything I don't want to do, especially if I might fail at it. This would be devastating.* Consequently, when asked to step up, many young people tend to resist.

I see this pattern regularly in my work with kids, teens and young adults. *Why should I do homework? It's stupid.* They don't care that it is an expectation of the teacher. If they can find a way to get a passing grade without doing homework, they will do it. If they don't feel like going to school, they won't. Never mind that having an education is an expectation in society. If it doesn't make sense to kids, it doesn't matter what society expects. Applying pressure only makes them resist more.

Getting kids to step up today requires more than veiled threats or bribery. These may work short-term, but do not address the deeper problem. Parents have to understand the underlying dynamics that contribute to the oppositional behavior. Some, which I described earlier, have to do with how some kids perceive their relationship with their parents.

Other factors include anxiety, inferiority, academic intruders such as ADHD, dyslexia, sensory integration problems, or learning challenges. The cognitive and emotional distortions kids develop about themselves and school can become deeply embedded in their thinking. Getting trapped in a power struggle with their parents reinforces their perception and the problem worsens.

Let me illustrate how this would work with a mom and her daughter who are in the early stages of a power struggle over homework completion. Following the two-step approach, the mother in this case would step in to learn from her daughter what makes the homework a problem. The attitude is one of concern without anxiety or anger. In essence, the mom needs to assume a stress-reducing position. Commenting on what she sees and asking questions with curiosity is a good place to start. "I can see you became angry when I instructed you to do your homework. Can you help me understand what you are angry about?"

Taking a non-threatening, concerned approach reduces the tension in the interaction and signals to her daughter that she cares about her feelings of discomfort. This has the potential of lowering anger in the child—which is likely a secondary emotion—and creating safety for her daughter to disclose the primary emotion which might be anxiety about performance. The parent can continue the process of stepping in by normalizing and soothing the child's anxiety. Once anxiety is reduced and a plan to attempt the homework is sketched out, the mother can step back and allow her daughter to step up to the task. The parent can remain in the background for support should the anxiety reappear, all the while maintaining a calm demeanor and instilling confidence in the child's ability to manage her feelings and complete the homework. The child may try to pull the parent into the old dance by being oppositional. However, as long as the mother remains calm, firm, and supportive, the chances are greater that her daughter will eventually step up and perform the task of homework.

Where Do You Need To Start?

When it comes to bringing respect back into your family, where do you need to start? For some, the answer to this question may seem daunting. The depth of disrespect is so apparent that it seems like the family needs an overhaul. You are not alone. Trust me when I say there is an epidemic of disrespect in many households today. So, take a deep breath and look again at the question of where to begin.

A key place to begin is modeling respect. What are your kids catching from your behavior? Do you explode when you are angry? Do you swear? Do you do the silent treatment when you are mad at someone? Do you simply go off on them? Kids are button pushers and they seem to know exactly when to push. What are you going to do about your buttons?

Modeling respect requires setting good boundaries, knowing how to regulate your emotions, modifying your attitude, and controlling your behavior. If this is difficult for you, then I recommend you review and implement all the procedures I outline in chapter three on bringing your self-respect back. In other words, you need to work on yourself before you know how to work on them.

Deactivating your buttons is not as difficult as it may seem. A good place to start is by learning stress relaxation exercises. These will help slow things down for you mentally and emotionally, which will help with keeping your cool in conflict. Modifying your use of language with your kids will also help in modeling respect. Statements that begin with *"You need to..."* are usually met with resistance and may ignite a conflict. Here are some examples of how you can communicate your message by modifying your language:

You need to change your attitude.
"It would be helpful if you could work on a more pleasant attitude."
You need to get your homework done.
"After you finish your homework, you can go back to playing your video game."
You need to listen to what I am saying.
"I would like for you to listen to what I am saying."

Modeling respect by how you interact with your kids gives them something to imitate as they watch you repeatedly handle challenging situations without losing your cool. Brandon eventually turned around when he saw that his parents were consistent in their respectful behavior toward each other, him, and Stacy. Patterns can change—it takes commitment, consistency, and time.

In the next chapter, I will introduce the concept of influential parenting. It is based on the two-step, one-step parent-child dance, and includes principles in parenting that are helpful in one of two ways: either establishing a culture of respect in a new family with little children, or changing a culture in a family with established patterns of disrespect. The good news coming from modern research indicates that behavioral change is possible! Science demonstrates how the neural-plasticity of the brain enables it to change patterns of thought and behavior. New neuronal brain patterns can be developed as individuals work on learning new ways of thinking and acting. I demonstrated this with the Hughes family. Albeit fictional, this family typifies families I help in my counseling practice who want to change unhealthy relational patterns. It can begin with a single individual, then a couple, and finally a whole family can embrace a different lifestyle based on respectful relationships.

Chapter Six

Influential Parenting: How to Get Your Kids to Step Up

Raising a family is not a walk in the park. It's more like a sprint. Try taking your kids for a walk in the park and you'll know what I mean. You need eyes in the back of your head as they scurry in different directions. Jenny wants to ride the slide while Steven heads toward the swings. Then there's your puddle-jumping kid Jason, who heads for the water fountain, but not for a drink. His creative little mind has transformed it into a weapon of mass destruction. Pressing his thumb partially into the hole, he shoots water like a scud missile on anyone who comes within range.

No sooner are you settled in to the playground when it turns into a battlefield. First, you hear the cry of your daughter pleading for help. You turn toward the sound and see wailing Jenny lying on the ground at the bottom of the slide. Posing at the top with a devilish grin is Steven who "volunteered" to push his sister down the slide. You fume toward the slide to attend to Jenny and give Steven a piece of your mind. Jenny dusts herself off, takes a quick hug and beelines to the fountain to clean the dirt off her hands, while you dole out Steven's punishment. Just at the moment you think you have restored calm, Jenny reaches the fountain and finds Jarhead Jason waiting for her, armed and ready to fire!

Parenting is the biggest responsibility in the world. From the time a baby is born until it launches into adulthood, parents have their work cut for them. Upon delivery, the proud parents are not given a manual to teach them how to raise children. It doesn't make sense to me that we require education and testing to obtain a driver's license, professional credentials, or gun ownership. However the two most important responsibilities, marriage and parenting, require no prior training.

So, where does one learn the skills of parenting? For most people, parenting styles are internalized from their family-of-origin. In other words, rookie parents do what they watched their parents do, even if they vowed they would never do it that way. Go figure. Generation after generation of individuals enter parenthood without a manual. The blind leading the blind.

When I was a child, getting kids to step up was fairly simple. If a kid protested a parent's command with a "Why?" the response was, "Because I said so!" No argument. No debate. The child was expected to obey, no questions asked. Any resistance was immediately met with some form of punishment: spanking, grounding, extra chores, or all the above. Kids stepped up because they did not want to face the consequences of disobeying their parents. Parents enforced consequences. There was also a respect factor toward parents that kept behavior in check for the most part.

I'm not suggesting a return to a form of authoritarian parenting; that would be an extreme swing of the pendulum. Besides, there are some elements of this parenting style that are not conducive to building respectful relationships. Compliance did not always come out of respect for parents, but often out of fear. Fearing parents does not equate to respecting parents. Nor does, "Because I said so" show respect to a child or teen who is asking a question. A more effective approach is one that balances the authoritative role of parents with age-appropriate autonomy necessary in child and adolescent development. I call this style influential parenting. This approach originates as far back as our genealogical roots begin. For me, it dates back to the Garden of Eden.

Some people consider religious teachings a manual for parenting. For example, people of Judeo-Christian faith view the sacred writings of the Torah or Bible as a source of inspiration and instruction. Those of a Muslim faith would look to the Quran as a resource for parenting. People from a Buddhist background might consider the teachings of Siddhartha Gautama as a guide. As a Christian, I turn to the Bible as my primary source on how to govern my personal life and interpersonal relationships.

Recently, I was reading the book of Genesis and uncovered in the Garden of Eden an interesting model for raising a family. No, there wasn't a secret numerical code that revealed a hidden message on parenting. I simply observed how the Creator established a living environment for his created, in this case Adam and Eve. Moreover, the interpersonal relationships illustrated what would work well in a family. I also found some fascinating principles I think would apply to an influential parenting approach. Indulge me and perhaps you can see how useful this design can be for your family, whether you are religious or not.

The principles in this model generalize to people who subscribe to spiritual values and those who do not. As you read, note the following representations: God the parent, Adam and Eve the children.

Principle #1: Influential Parents Instill A Sense Of Value In Their Children.

In the Garden of Eden, we meet the first family, God's finale in a week of magnificent creative performances. Every day, the Creator designed something new and different. At the end of the day, he would look at what he created and say, "It is good." He waited until the sixth day to create man. It was to be the last and the best of all he made.

"Let us create man in our own image."

That's what God did. He made male and female beings in his likeness. When he finished creating humans, he stepped back and looked at all he had made and said something different. He said, *"It is very good."*

Here we find the first principle in God's model for the family: He instilled a sense of value in his creation. God observed inherent goodness in his children made in his likeness and they mattered to him.

As parents, we are also creators of life. Value is inherent in every child conceived in a mother's womb. Every child born is a unique gift of life delicately and artistically designed. If you've adopted children, you may not have created them, but you have chosen to care for a human being, someone of tremendous value to you and God.

The youngest in my family, my brother Tom, was born prematurely in my mother's seventh month of pregnancy. The umbilical cord was wrapped around his throat, causing a lack of oxygen to his brain, resulting in brain damage. The effects of this condition left him with a mental disability, exhibited in verbal and motor skill deficits. Never did my parents consider Tom less valuable than his four siblings. On the contrary,

Tom brought added value to our family because of his innocence, kindness, and love toward every person he met.

The value God instilled in his firstborn children is evident in how he interacted with them. He spent time with them walking in the garden, "in the cool of the day." Relationship was a priority, so he made time for them. He also instilled value by giving them a sense of purpose and autonomy to rule the earth.

God valued his children in good times and in bad times. When they disobeyed him and went into hiding, God went looking for them. He handled the situation in a way that did not diminish the seriousness of the offense, but preserved their dignity. Adam and Eve hid in the bushes and covered their nakedness with leaves because they felt shame. However, God did not shame them; rather, he helped them deal appropriately with their shame. More on that later.

Is there a lesson here for parents? Pay attention to the message you send to your kids about their self-worth. Kids have intrinsic value because they are acts of creation and should be treated with dignity at all times. It is important that you see it and never lose sight of it. Communicate it to them in words and actions. A child's self-concept is initially formed by the messages they receive and internalize in the early stages of life from their primary caregivers. It is important that they feel loved and accepted by you. What is more important, they need to know you love them in good times and in bad, like when they break one of your rules or disappoint you.

Shame may also lead your kids to feel bad about themselves and hide from you. They may lie, make excuses, or blame others for their behavior. Or, having acknowledged fault, your kid may feel like they've failed you as a son or daughter. How you handle the situation will have an effect on how they see themselves and what they will learn from their choices.

How do you separate behavior you disapprove of from a teenager you love? First, you must balance enforcing consequences with dispensing grace. Consequences are important so that kids learn from bad decisions. A responsible parent will be sure to enforce consequences to shape appropriate behavior. However, what follows consequences is equally important to the child. Showing your kids love and forgiveness conveys the message that they matter to you. Receiving your forgiveness will help them to forgive themselves and not be enslaved by shame. A shame core is detrimental to a healthy self-image and lays the foundation for addictions and other forms of self-destructive behavior.

Principle #2: Influential Parents Are The Primary Providers Of Their Kids' Needs

In the garden, God made full provisions to meet the basic needs of the first family. Rich vegetation and fruit-bearing trees gave them plenty of nutritious food to eat. God had taken care of their physical needs. The garden was their home, a place of their own where they could live and thrive. The conditions were ideal for them not just to survive but to produce an expansive offspring. God created the ideal environment for a growing family! So he said, *"Be fruitful and multiply…"*

The first family's needs were not relegated to food and shelter. The Creator designed human beings to exist in relationship, a characteristic of being created in the image of God. Adam and Eve, the prototype, were created to live in interpersonal relationships with each other and their Maker. In the Genesis account, we discover that God walked with the couple in the evening. What's the point? He did not place them alone in the garden, leaving them to find their own way. God spent time with them in relationship.

Human beings are meant to live in relationships. "It is not good for man to be alone." Interpersonal relationship is a basic human need. This is how we are wired. The development of self does not happen in isolation; it occurs in relationship with others. In a family, a child's sense of self is formed by verbal and nonverbal messages received from his or her primary caretakers. Throughout the stages of human development, these messages are internalized and shape one's view of self. The absence of healthy attachment deprives a child of a basic human need to feel connected to others. Consequently, the child may struggle being connected to self.

The concept of man's basic need for human and divine connection is now being supported in scientific research.[7] The Commission of Chil-

---

7   For more information visit: www.americanvalues.org

dren at Risk is a committee of over thirty mental health professionals and brain researchers. After exhaustive research and collaboration, they made the following statement:

> In the midst of unprecedented material affluence, the deteriorating mental and behavioral health of U.S. children, high and rising rates of depression, anxiety, attention deficit, conduct disorders, thoughts of suicide, and other serious mental, emotional, and behavioral problems among U.S. children and adolescents, we as a society are thinking about this deterioration, our failure to recognize the broad environmental conditions that are contributing to growing numbers of suffering children. The cause of this crisis of American childhood is a lack of connectedness, close connections to other people, and deep connections to moral and spiritual meaning.

This empirical study gives evidence of how brain development and sense of self is in direct correlation to the quality of attachment an infant has with its primary caregiver. Furthermore, it shows how the parent-child relationship is the basis for learning, not only basic tasks such as talking, but emotional processes and moral and spiritual development.

As we examine the garden model, we discover God is both creator and parent of the first family. He is the primary provider of their physical and relational needs. Following this model, parents are the primary providers of their kids' needs. Physical needs include basic things like shelter, food, and protection. However, it doesn't end there. Influential parents also meet their kids' relational needs. This means being available to your kids and spending quality time with them.

Kids crave meaningful connection with their parents. In times of interaction, parents model how to express a full range of emotions: love, joy, laughter, sadness, anger, and compassion. Some of my earliest childhood recollections are memory flashes of my mom reaching down to take me out of a playpen and cradle me in her arms to sing me a lullaby. Her soft voice and tender arms calmed my anxiety and quieted my soul.

I also remember when I was five or six years old, snuggling next to my dad on the couch, listening to the Chicago Bears on the radio. This was in the days when Bears games were blacked out from television because the stadium didn't sell out. Dad would shout with excitement when Gayle Sayers ran for touchdown or yell in frustration at an interception. Dad's mood was often determined by the final score of the game. Unfortunately, back then the Bears had more losing seasons than winning ones!

I'll never forget the first time I had to get stitches. I was about 5 years old when I split my lip open after a nasty fall. My dad, the stoic Swede, didn't show much emotion, so I was a really anxious when I heard he was taking me to the hospital. The last thing I needed was an emotionally unavailable father telling me to "toughen up, Son." Instead, I have a vivid memory of peering into my dad's eyes through the surgical cloth while he held my hand. I was able to muster up the courage to lay motionless on the operating table without Novocain while the doctor delicately stitched my upper lip because my dad assured me I could do it and he would stay by my side. Later, dad told me he was proud of me and promised me to take me for an ice-cream cone after the stitches were out. He delivered on his promise, too! It was one of those rare bonding moments I had with my dad.

Principle #3: Influential Parents, Give Their Kids A Sense Of Purpose.

When God created the first family, he placed his DNA in them. They were like him in many ways. They had creative ability. They were given authority to rule over creation. God gave them a purpose that included personal responsibility. First, he said, *"Be fruitful and multiply."* Create more life. Have children. Populate the planet. *"Fill the earth and subdue it."* Furthermore, he instructed the first family to rule over the creatures of the earth. They were given the responsibility to name the animals and to rule over them. They were given hierarchy in the created order and autonomy to govern. Thus, to compliment the value he instilled in his children, he gave them a purpose to fulfill.

Can you imagine the confidence they gained by hearing God give them this assignment? The message, if we can read between the lines, is *I have every confidence in your ability to handle this task, so I leave it in your hands.* There's a secondary message in the assignment. They understood that being a member of God's family meant making a personal contribution to maintain order and balance.

If I understand the garden model correctly, individuals are created with a purpose in life. Influential parents understand this and prepare their children by instilling confidence in them at a very early age. They train their kids to handle age-appropriate responsibility by giving them little tasks to do, simple things like putting their toys away, helping set the table, or emptying the wastebaskets.

When I was little, my daily chore was taking out the trash. My dad showed me how to do it and watched me a few times to make sure I got it right. Once I did, he left me on my own to do it. It meant a lot to me for dad to trust me to take the trash out by myself. I felt like one of my older siblings because I was making a contribution to the family. At the end of the week, I stood in line with the others to get my allowance. It was a big deal.

As I got older though, the novelty of having a chore wore off. After a while, it became a pain in my little behind. To make a boring job interesting, I would pretend that the bag of garbage was really a disguised bomb I was depositing in enemy territory.

One day, as I was going through the battle zone, I pretended I was shot and fell on the ground writhing in pain and agony. As I lay there, I heard this laughter coming from the back door of our house. Sure enough, it was my parents and siblings laughing out loud, yet somewhat perplexed by this bizarre display. After I explained my imaginary game, they laughed even harder. Needless to say, I was given an extended tour of duty as the garbage disposer, a.k.a. special force ranger.

Today, many parents seem reluctant to give their kids responsibility. Instead, they do things their kids should be doing for themselves. In the Garden Model, belonging needs were met by making a contribution to the family. The Creator knew their potential; he simply created opportunities for them to use it by giving them responsibilities in the garden.

Influential parents are not afraid to give their kids tasks to do in the family. Furthermore, they instill confidence in their kids by providing opportunities for them to try. Remember, kids internalize these messages and it influences how they see themselves. Parental confidence breeds self-confidence. On the other hand, parents who criticize their children or always point out their faults send a strong message of incompetence. Kids will perform in a manner that matches the message. Think about what and how you communicate with your kids.

By giving your kids age-appropriate chores, you lay the groundwork for a healthy work ethic that will serve them well throughout their development from childhood to adulthood. With each success, their self-confidence and self-esteem flourishes. As they progress through the normal developmental stages, they learn more about themselves, what interests them, and discover latent talents and skills. Their sense of self becomes more clearly defined as they discern what is and what is not them. Over the course of time, they discover a purpose for their lives.

Parents, when you give kids chores, there are a few simple rules to keep in mind. First, before you assign the chore, teach them how to do it. If my dad told me to take out the garbage without showing me how to do it, I might have placed it in the garden or on the neighbor's lawn. Instead, he showed me how to secure it, carry it out, where to place it, and how to replace the old bag with a new one. This may sound elementary to you, but some parents forget this first rule and become frustrated with kids when they don't perform to their expectations. The problem is that the kids didn't know what these expectations are because they weren't explained, nor demonstrated.

Second, be patient and encourage your kids as they learn a new skill. Your responses will have either a positive or negative effect on them. Frustration, impatience, and irritability do not instill confidence in kids. Conversely, it makes them feel anxious, incompetent, and they will likely avoid doing the task.

Finally, once you delegate responsibility, give them time to do it on their own. Give oversight from a distance. In other words, don't hover over them. If they don't do the job correctly, don't scold them. Rather, comment on what they did right, and show them where they can make improvement. Remember to keep a positive attitude as you train them.

Sometimes, kids will challenge your rules. They may not follow through on what you ask them to do. When this occurs, you will need to step in and enforce a consequence so that they can learn from their choices. With consistent effort on your part to oversee their work and to give out appropriate consequences, you should see their behavior improve.

One final thought about the principle of instilling a sense of purpose in your kids. As the primary caretaker of your children, you have the perfect vantage point to observe their development and potential in life. You may see early on their interest in such things as music, art, sports, or science. Over time, you discover they have natural ability that matches their interest. As an influential parent, you will want to pay attention to this and encourage their interests. Help them understand that these traits are encoded in them for a purpose. This will likely give them a sense of direction. Be supportive without pushing them. While you may point out what you see as their potential, they will need to see it for themselves in order for it to become an internalized interest or passion.

Principle #4: Influential Parents Establish Structure In Their Family

In the Garden of Eden, God established physical and moral boundaries. The physical boundaries included the four rivers that bordered the Garden of Eden. You can read about this in the Genesis account. There is no indication that they were not permitted beyond these aquatic borders. In fact, as they populated the earth, it was assumed they would venture beyond the garden. Suffice it to say that in the early days, the garden was their home. The physical boundaries included fruit-bearing trees for food. They were also told what was off-limits. Only the tree of the knowledge of good and evil was off the list. Here, we observe a moral boundary.

The first family was placed in an environment where their basic needs were met and where they could flourish and have dominion in the earth. Within this structure, God gave them autonomy to rule. It included clearly defined expectations—some would say rules—about how they were to live in it. These expectations included things we discussed earlier, populating the earth and having dominion over the animal and plant life. They were given freedom within limits. This is an important concept as you think about establishing structure in your family.

The freedom within limits structure came with an expectation: *"You *are free to eat from any tree in the garden, but you must not eat from the tree of the knowledge of good and evil, for when you eat of it you will surely die"* (Genesis 2:16,17). Notice the emphasis was on freedom, independence, latitude, opportunity, authority, and power. The structure he established gave them room to grow on their own with plenty of opportunity to flourish.

However, he also established a moral boundary they were told not to cross. The forbidden fruit hanging from the tree of the knowledge of good and evil was off limits. He warned them of the consequences they would face if they acted outside the boundaries he marked: *"...for when you eat of it you will surely die."* At the time, physical death did not exist in the human race. Well, we know what happened in the next episode of this reality series. Adam and Eve ate the forbidden fruit. They crossed the moral boundary and faced the consequences of their actions. I will address the implications shortly.

When it comes to structure in families, influential parents also establish physical and moral boundaries for their children. Physical boundaries focus on personal space and geographical limits. Moral boundaries clarify right and wrong behavior. Structure is taught early on and adjusted as children develop maturity and increase their ability to manage themselves.

This model teaches us another important lesson on parenting. While it is the job of parents to provide a proper structure for their children and to instruct them on the expectations of living in the family, it must be balanced with autonomy, giving kids opportunity to grow by making decisions. It's called personal responsibility. You cannot protect your kids from danger by keeping them in a bubble. They will never develop self-reliance if they depend on their parents to make decisions for them, or to rescue them from poor decisions. Adam and Eve knew the rules within the structure that God set up for them. In the end they made a wrong decision. They acted outside of the boundary he had established. The consequences they faced taught them some valuable lessons going forward.

Here is a critical stage in parenting. You've established structure in your family, composed of rules and expectations on how to live together. Furthermore, you've explained beforehand what the consequences will be if the rules are violated. Eventually, one of the kids disobeys the rules and thereby tests the limits you've established. Now comes the unpleasant moment when you have to decide what you're going to do.

In the garden account, the Creator models for us the appropriate parental response. He enforces the consequences he has previously outlined. These consequences are heavy, yet he knows that they will not learn unless he enforces them.

Imagine if he did not follow through on his warning. In future situations, they would attribute his warnings to idle threats and not take him seriously. Furthermore, they would challenge his authority at every turn until the physical and moral structures were destroyed and anarchy ruled.

This is precisely what happens in families when parents fail to establish structure with consequences. Before long, kids don't take them seriously. They challenge their authority by doing their own thing. Over time, the hierarchical structure is inverted, with the kids on the top and the parents on the bottom. This is too much power for kids and leaves them feeling anxious on the inside, although you would never notice by their behavior. The bottom line is that in order for kids to feel safe in a family, their parents have to establish some form of structure with clearly defined boundaries and communicated expectations about appropriate behavior.

Principle #5: Influential Parents Provide Moral And Spiritual Guidance For Their Kids

Thus far, we've learned that in the garden model, the Creator instilled a sense of value in people, along with a sense of purpose. We also discovered that he was the primary provider for their physical and relational needs. Next, we learned that he established a structure with physical and moral boundaries so that they could have freedom within limits. Before we close the chapter on influential parenting, we have one more lesson to learn, which has to do with moral development.

In the first two chapters of Genesis, everything seemed to be going well for the first family. They were given everything they needed to live and prosper on the earth. They also enjoyed a shared intimate relationship with their Creator, walking with him during the cool of the day. Created in the image of their Maker, they reflected the innocence of their

Godlike nature. Genesis records their appearance: *"The man and his wife were both naked, and they felt no shame."*

Things were going well until the couple lingered by the tree with forbidden fruit. Here, the crafty serpent offered them some fruit. Deceived by the serpent, the couple ate the fruit. In this simple act, they crossed the moral boundary and sin entered their hearts. For the first time, they felt ashamed inwardly and outwardly. They hid in the bushes and attempted to cover their nakedness, hence their shame.

Later in the day, when God appeared to walk with them, the couple was missing. In his search, he called out to them, only to find them hiding in the bushes, afraid to see him because of their shame. This tragic moment depicts a breach of trust, a ruptured relationship and the consequences that follow.

After the consequences were served, the first family stood before their Creator. Hearts broken, fearful and ashamed, they waited for him to turn his back on them in utter rejection. It's an embarrassing moment to say the least. They were about to be totally abandoned by God.

Then something strange happens next. Before the gates are closed on the Garden of Eden he does something that they did not expect, something that never happened before. He sacrifices an animal and uses the skin to make clothing for the couple. The first act of shedding blood, resulting in death, was done to cover their shame. God did this act on their behalf to cover the shame they could not erase on their own. God sent a message of forgiveness and the restoration of their relationship with God. Furthermore, it established a precedent that God is a reconciler of broken relationships.

You may be wondering how this relates to parenting. Let me try to weave this into a logical pattern. First, a significant test in your relationship with your children will occur when they cross the boundaries you establish for them. Whether it be lying, stealing, cheating, or some other violation, you are in a position to take some form of action. How you respond to your kids will determine the course of your relationship with them.

When kids are young, parents tend to be more understanding and forgiving. However, as they get older and smarter, when they have fewer excuses to hide behind, their misbehavior may be harder to justify. Furthermore, if they are teenagers having problems with their parents, the situation becomes more challenging to sort out.

In most cases, when kids do wrong, they feel ashamed. They may conclude you don't love them, especially when they see you are angry. Shaming kids because you're embarrassed by their behavior and how it makes you look will only make matters worse. First of all, their behavior may be intended to embarrass you as payback for how they think you make them feel. If they feel unloved, unwanted, or unaccepted, they may act out in anger. Shaming them because you are embarrassed only fuels their anger and intensifies the battle.

So, how do you balance parental authority with unconditional love? To answer this, let's go back to the garden for a moment. Here, God is clearly angry and disappointed with his children for their inappropriate behavior. He warned them what would happen if they crossed the line and he enforced the consequences when they did it. End of story.

Well, not exactly. He did not despise them, making them feel worse than they already felt. Their shame and embarrassment was obvious. Their feeble attempt to correct their problem by covering their nakedness with fig leaves was not working either.

Here's what God does and this is the lesson parents can learn. He separated what they did from who they were. He punished their behavior. Next, he forgave them and restored his relationship with them by covering their shame. In essence, he was saying, "I forgive you." The message was clearly intended to restore their relationship and remove the shame they felt.

Internalization of parental messages is a major part of identity formation. Kids internalize the messages they receive—positive or negative, good or bad. When they act in ways that bring shame upon themselves and disappoint parents, it is a critical moment in their development. Consequences must be enforced. In the end, they need to know that they are forgiven, that they are loved, and that they are not rejected. Parents who hold onto their anger and take things too personally will shame their kids.

Kids may develop an internalized shame core that will influence how they see themselves. However, when parents communicate to their children that they are forgiven and loved apart from their behavior, they are more likely to learn three important things. First, they will learn to respect the boundaries established and modify their behavior. Second, knowing they are loved unconditionally, they will not develop a shame core; they'll have a healthy self-identity. Third, they will develop a secure attachment with their parents. The balance of love and limits creates a sense of safety in the protective and loving care of their parents. This will foster healthy growth and identity formation throughout the developmental stages, from birth to adulthood.

Introducing your children to vital spirituality—to a belief in the goodness of God—is the most powerful way you can influence a healthy development of your children's sense of self. Teaching your children about God will expose them to divine attributes of unconditional love, intrinsic value, forgiveness, grace, and purpose in life. Introducing your children to spiritual practices of prayer, the reading of scripture, and serving others will help shape their view of themselves in the world.

As you can see, parenting is an enormous task with little or no advanced training. Many parents feel intimidated by the task and suffer enormous guilt, fearing they will damage their kids if they don't get it right. Perhaps you feel this way too. If so, you are not alone. In my work, I talk to many parents who struggle with feelings of worry and guilt. I remind them that making mistakes is simply a part of learning to be an influential parent. Much like you want your kids to learn from their wrong choices, you can learn from yours. If you forgive your children when they do wrong, they will likely forgive you when you make mistakes.

In the previous chapter, I talked about the dance parents and kids engage in that exhibits respect. Parents do the two-step: step in and step back, followed by kids who do the one-step: step up. Engaging kids in this dance of respect is not as easy as it sounds. One of the key elements in this dance is having an awareness of personal power. Another involves instilling values in kids when they are young. Let's take a closer look at how this works in the final two principles of influential parenting.

Principle # 6: Influential Parents Respect Personal Power

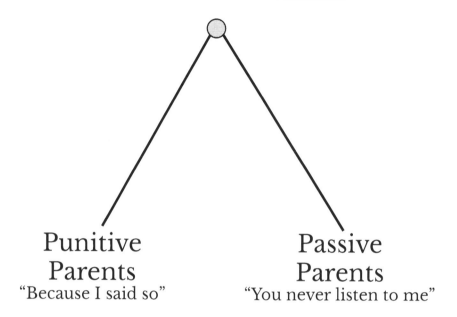

Picture a pendulum. On one end, we have punitive parenting, a style prominent a generation ago. It was an authoritarian, my way or the highway approach that made kids fear their parents. On the other end of the pendulum is passive parenting, the don't-rock-the-boat approach based on parents' fear of their kids. As I indicated previously, these extremes do not work. In the middle of the pendulum is a more favorable approach: influential parenting. This style of parenting strikes a balance in the following areas:
- Authority and autonomy
- Love and limits

- Confidence and competency
- Failure and forgiveness.

Influential parents know how to use their power to inspire children in the use of their power. Power regulates all human relationships. Power consists of an individual's ability to think, feel, and act for themselves. When two or more people are together, a power dynamic exists. Healthy relationships honor an individual's right to power—thinking, feeling, choosing—at all times.

Underlying this respect of power is an understanding of the uniqueness of an individual's subjective experience of life. This includes factors of personality, temperament, intelligence, characteristics, and abilities. A universal lens does not exist. This explains why kids growing up in the same home will have different interpretations of family life based on their subjective experience.

In parent-child relationships, a balance of power weighs more heavily on the side of parents, for obvious reasons. Therefore, in terms of power status, parents outrank their children. Even so, parents have a responsibility to use their power in a manner to protect, provide, nurture, and guide their children. Furthermore, parents also use their power to inspire their children to flourish as they grow from infancy to adulthood. Overuse of power by parents by dominating their children can hinder their growth and identity formation. Underuse of power by being passive or permissive can also stymie their development.

Influential parents encourage the development of their children's power in age-appropriate expressions. For example, they understand as an infant transitions to a toddler, he or she will use their power to explore their little universe. Influential parents don't meet the child's expressions of No or Mine with harsh reactions; they choose thoughtful responses that introduce limits without smothering self-expression.

When interacting with their children, influential parents exhibit respect by encouraging them to talk, listening carefully to what they have to say, responding in a manner that conveys understanding, and giving clear answers that kids can understand. "Because I said so" is not a clear answer; it is merely a power play. Repetitions of this style will set the parent-child relationship up for a power struggle.

Remember, a goal in influential parenting is to encourage, not discourage the use of a child's power. An influential parent will respond to the *Why* question by addressing the thinking and feeling reactions of their children. Here's an example of this style in the Hughes' family.

STACY

Hey mom, I'm going out tonight with Heather and Lizzie to see the new Twilight movie.

HEIDI

Sorry Stace, but I am going to veto your plans.

STACY:

Why?

HEIDI:

Because you already agreed to babysit for the Franklins.

STACY

Yeah but, this is the premiere showing! They can get someone else to babysit.

HEIDI

You made a commitment to the Franklins and it is important for you to keep it.

STACY

This is stupid! You're not being fair, Mom.

HEIDI

I can see you are angry. It doesn't seem fair to you to have to miss this event with your friends. However, sometimes things don't always work out the way we want. Tonight is one of those times. On the flip side, you will be keeping your word, which is like gold. You will also be making money. The movie will be showing tomorrow. If you want, I will go with you to see it, or you can go with some other friends.

STACY

Whatever!

HEIDI

I understand you're disappointed. Think about my offer. It might be fun to go together.

Notice how Heidi avoided a power struggle by maintaining her cool, holding her position, and responding to Stacy on both levels: thinking and feeling. First, she explained why Stacy could not go to the movies. However, she didn't end there. Heidi also addressed the emotions Stacy felt, validating and normalizing them. This allowed Stacy to express how she felt about her mother's decision without Heidi pulling rank and shutting her down. It was also a lesson about commitments and being responsible to others. Knowing Stacy would get over her feelings, Heidi used her authority to train her daughter to be a responsible teenager. This brings us to the seventh principle of influential parenting.

Principle #7: Influential Parents Instill Social Values

Power without principles produces problems! Children need to learn how to navigate their world in a manner that does not get them into trouble in the exercise of their power. Here is where influential parents play an important role in instilling a value of respect in their kids. They teach their children to value both independence and interdependence. Independence has to do with personal responsibility. Interdependence is about social responsibility. Influential parents teach their children how their choices affect themselves and others. Furthermore, they help their kids to think ahead before they act.

Children must learn social awareness. Kids need to understand the cause and effect dynamic in social interaction, whether it be at home with parents and siblings, or in larger social systems like school, church, or sports. Respect is the element that makes these interactions successful and rewarding. Training children how to show respect to others will help them relate socially and develop good friendships.

For this to occur, the cause-and-effect dynamic must be learned first at home. To this end, influential parents introduce their children to basic rules of engagement that foster respect. These rules incorporate boundaries, reciprocity, communication, and accommodation. Take a look at some rules and the values that drive them.

Value #1: We respect our relationships.
1. We will accept the uniqueness of every individual member of the family.

2. We will avoid doing harm to each other by words or actions that hurt.
3. We will seek to be kind, helpful, and loving toward each other.

Value #2: We respect each other's personal space.
1. We will avoid hitting each other when angry.
2. We will not take each other's things without asking.
3. We will honor a person's request for space.
4. We will ask before we enter a person's bedroom.

Value #3: We respect each other when talking.
1. We will listen carefully when spoken to.
2. We will speak respectfully when responding.
3. When we have a conflict, we will try to resolve it fairly.
4. When we disagree, we will respect our differences.
5. When we act disrespectfully, we will repair our offenses with the other person.

Value #4: We respect our home.
1. We will respect our parents as the leaders of our family.
2. We will respect each other as brothers and sisters.
3. We will respect our home by making a contribution to keep it clean.
4. We will cooperate with our parents and siblings by working together.
5. We will not act in a way that violates the values of our family.

Teaching these values in the home when your children are young will lay the groundwork for a respectful family and successful social relationships. Instilling values and shaping behavior is easier when children are young and impressionable. Attempting to establish these values when kids are older is like turning around an ocean liner. It takes time and commitment. As I stated previously, older kids will meet you with resistance when you try to change the culture of your home to value respect. Knowing this, you will have to be patient, persistent, and somewhat creative in your approach. Older teens may laugh at the rules of engagement listed above. You may need to convey the message with language that resounds with them.

Three Key Things To Remember About Influential Parents

Before I conclude this chapter, let me highlight three key elements of influential parenting:

The ability to instill something of value in their children.
- Instillation of intrinsic worth in the child: You matter.
- Installation of competency in the child: You have unique abilities.
- Installation of confidence in the child: *I believe you can.*
- Installation of values in the child: *This is what we believe and why.*

The ability to balance love and limits.
- Conveying a sense of unconditional love to the child
- Expressing love in words and actions
- Establishing clearly defined boundaries
- Educating the child on the reason for the limits
- Enforcing consequences when the limits are violated

The ability to respect and encourage the use of personal power.
- Recognizing autonomy as a normal process of the child's development from toddlerhood to adulthood
- Respecting the child's need to exercise personal power
- Encouraging the child's expression of thoughts, feelings, and behavior within an age-appropriate manner
- Enforcing boundaries with the child when the expression of personal power moves outside the age-appropriate range of expression

These three key elements are what set influential parents apart from the rest of the pack. They understand the power of instilling virtues in their children. Influential parents keep love and limits in balance so their children do not develop distorted views of their self-worth. They are acutely aware of the power dynamic in the parent-child relationship and encourage the appropriate expression of their children's autonomy. Doing these things well and with consistency will establish a respectful culture in the home.

Chapter Seven

Bringing Respect Back in the Workplace

KEVIN ROLLS OUT of bed a little easier these days. Ever since he and Heidi have made an effort to focus on their relationship, things have been improving at home. Communication is more respectful and they seem to have less to fight about these days. When conflicts occur, they do a much better job resolving issues rather than stockpiling them. Now that they have less to argue about, they seem to have more time to connect. The gazebo, once an escape for Kevin, has become a retreat for the couple to relax together and talk.

Lately, Kevin has been sharing with Heidi his struggles at work.

KEVIN
The problem isn't simply a lack of communication. That's secondary. What's missing is a lack of connection—top to bottom. Our structure is your typical corporate topdown ladder. The people on the top seem more interested in knowing the bottom line than the people on the bottom rung. Our employees want less work and more benefits. That's not going to happen. So, relationships are based on performance and this creates a competitive tone among coworkers. So what we have is a dog-eat-dog mentality with a lack of trust, top to bottom.

HEIDI
It sounds like you are trapped between two sets of expectations. It is an awful position to be placed in Kevin. No doubt, it is taken a toll on you. You are doing the best you can. Unfortunately, upper man-

agement does not get the bigger picture. If you think it is time for you to make a career change, I will support you honey.

Kevin relates the pressure he feels from upper management to increase production and profits for the company while simultaneously hearing employees clamor for easier workload and more entitlements. Neither the top nor the bottom trust each other has their best interests in mind. They place the burden of responsibility on Kevin, the middle manager, to execute their agenda. The bosses want him to communicate the vision, motivate the team, and lower costs by cutting back on the expenditures of employees. The employees want more help to keep up with the work demand and for the company to furnish iPads to help them get their job done more efficiently.

Company morale is further affected by interpersonal conflicts in the sales team over performance bonuses and among some of the clerical staff over disparity in workload. Fighting and bickering between departments threatens production and triggers the impatience of the executives.

With pressure coming from both sides, Kevin feels overwhelmed and powerless. When he talks with fellow mid-managers in other departments, they report similar problems. Recently, some of his colleagues left the company because they could not handle the stress of the job. Now, Kevin contemplates quitting too.

Heidi, who holds a similar position with the bank, understands Kevin's dilemma. She listens carefully as he unpacks the problem and responds empathically to his struggles. She knows Kevin is not a quitter, but she realizes the problem is systemic in nature and will not likely change unless upper management takes a different leadership approach. In the meantime, Heidi affirms Kevin's qualities as a manager, admires his perseverance, and encourages him to consider other options if he thinks it is time for a change.

Disrespect In The Workplace

Can you relate to Kevin? Perhaps you feel the squeeze from upper and lower tiers of the corporate structure. You don't have to be in a managerial position to understand his struggle. No one likes to work in an environment where people don't get along, act disrespectfully, and seem to look out for only themselves.

Think about it. Most of us spend the majority of our waking day at work eight or more hours per day. Imagine spending this amount of time in an environment where people don't enjoy being together. Maybe you don't have to imagine; maybe this describes your world of work. If so, it must be drudgery going through a day, as if it were some form of punishment. Several factors can contribute to an unsatisfactory work environment, yet one of the major offenders is interpersonal relations—how people get along.

I am a business owner and currently employ eight people at my counseling center. Over the forty years of my career path, I have had the opportunity to look at how work is conducted from a variety of perspectives. After my stint as a paper boy, I started my first job as a grocery bagger when I was sixteen years old. Over the ten years I worked in the grocery store, I went from a bagger, to stock clerk, and eventually assistant manager.

During the next twenty-five years of my career, I worked in pastoral ministry on various levels of service: youth minister, assistant minister, and eventually senior pastor. I also was elected and served in various leadership roles within the religious organization I was affiliated with during this time. What was unique about this phase of my career was the volume of volunteer workers required to staff the plethora of programs in the church. These were individuals who were not earning a paycheck for their service. At any time, they could walk away from their volunteer work for whatever reason: busyness, burnout, or perhaps a conflict of some sort. Creating a culture of respect was important to ensure volunteers were adequately supported in their work.

Currently, I a member in a group of business owners who meet monthly to learn from each other how we can be better leaders at work, home, and in other areas of influence. In comparison to fellow business owners, I operate a small, more manageable business. Some of my colleagues own companies that employ hundreds of people. My wife Marian also works as a regional vice-president of a large corporation. She oversees teams in fifteen states, with nearly fourteen thousand employees under her watch. In conversations with my wife and friends, I hear the common challenges businesses experience with employee relations.

Recently, I interviewed two of my friends who own their own businesses, about respect in the workplace. I also interviewed Marian to get her perspective on the issue of respect from an upper management level. In particular, I was interested in how important a culture of respect was to these owners of their companies.

What did they do to foster respect in the workplace? In their view, was there a correlation between respect and performance, respect and profit? If respect was a core value for the company, how did they cultivate it in the work environment? How important was it for them as owners to be shown respect? What did they do when respect was not being exhibited toward them or the company for that matter? Their answers to these questions are worth considering as you think about bringing respect back into the workplace.

John Pitzaferro, owner of TransNational Bankcard. From an early age, John developed a passion to start his own business. By 1999, John's entrepreneurial adventures led him to start a credit card processing business, TransNational Bankcard. Through hard work and long hours, the business grew, moving several times to accommodate its growth. TransNational Bankcard is currently located in Rosemont, Illinois, and has flourished into a nationwide recognition, a Chicago Tribune Top 100 Workplace two years in a row.

Scott Schnurr is the owner and CEO of DRF Trusted Property Solutions. Scott, a serial entrepreneur, started DRF in 2004, directing corporate growth over six hundred percent while adding four new divisions. He has cultivated relations with major Fortune 500 clients, creating industry-leading integrated business analytics and CRM platforms integral to driving consistent top performance in customer service and efficiencies.

In your experience as an owner and/or executive in business, is there a problem of respect in the work environment?

MARIAN
Mainly in the way individuals interact with each other. Problems are often mishandled by gossip or maligning an individual against

their superior or coworker to create a wrong impression. Lower-level employees observe what is going on and subsequently lose respect for both management and their game-playing coworkers.

JOHN

I prefer the word "challenge" over "problem." There is definitely a challenge in cultivating respect in our workplace. We all have heard that respect is something that must be earned. That said, we are all products of our upbringing and many kids have been raised in environments that do not teach or value respect. These children eventually grow up and enter the work force. They cannot practice what they have not learned. They can however, be taught respect in the work place. This can be done by rewarding respectful behaviors and reprimanding disrespectful behaviors. At our company, regardless of how financially successful an individual is, disrespect is not something we tolerate for very long. We put a higher value on our business family culture than we do on financial gain. Therefore, if an individual in our company does not want to play nice in our sandbox, they will not be allowed back in the sandbox!

SCOTT

The issue of respect in the workplace is as varied and unique from business to business as it is from family to family. The head of the household models behavior for the family. Heads of a company do the same. Furthermore, the behaviors manifested in a company typically mirror the executive's family life. Get it right at home and you will get it right at work. That being said, respect or lack of in both arenas is something that will always require vigilance and effort.

To what degree do you think a lack of respect impacts how a company conducts business?

MARIAN

A great degree. Employees that feel respect and see that leadership is healthy will be more engaged. Stronger teams will develop naturally and the end result will be increased productivity.

JOHN

Respect, or lack thereof, impacts every aspect of how a company conducts itself. 360-degree respect is the only acceptable standard. For example, if you respect your staff but not your clients, your staff sees and concludes that respect is based on economic factors. If the company's economic environment changes, staff knows you will disrespect them just as easily.

SCOTT

Looking at it from a leadership perspective, the business develops a personality and culture that follows the modeled behavior of leaders. This behavioral standard applies to everyone from team members and vendors to customers and the families of the business. As a business leader, you can't allow someone to act inappropriately in one segment of life and then expect them to apply a completely opposite set of values in another area. It just doesn't work.

How does this affect goals and objectives?

JOHN

If your staff does not feel valued or respected, they are not going to perform even near their level of capability. Therefore, they will not achieve the goals or objectives and will not feel fulfilled or content. Believe it or not, staff will perform at a much higher level, achieve more than they thought possible, and challenged to reach their God-given potential if they feel respected and valued. Without this feeling of fulfillment, high performance individuals will eventually decide to move out of that environment in search of one that values respect.

SCOTT

Goals and objectives are long term thoughts applied to a documented process. The values related to respect are what drive the goals and objectives. Without respect, the goals and objectives are self-centered and self-serving.

MARIAN

In this struggling economy, individuals are working harder and with less resources. The job market is tough. When employees are faced with dog-eat-dog behaviors at work, they focus on survival versus their work. This comes with a steep price when resources are already reduced. When respect is absent everything suffers: morale, production, productivity, and job satisfaction.

How is respect cultivated in a work environment? Who does what?

JOHN
You must have a nurturing and compassionate environment that rewards success and respect. Just as important, if not more so, you must address disrespect when it occurs. All your policies must be objective, not subjective, when it comes to disrespectful conduct. All the while, compassionately knowing that, most often, a disrespectful person is just a product of their upbringing and not a rotten apple. With proper training and accountability, they can learn to be a productive, fulfilled, and respectful member of your team. That is not to say there are not rotten apples. Stay in business for any amount of time and you will certainly bump into a rotten apple or two. The great news about rotten apples, they hate a truly wonderful work environment. If your culture is truly 360 degrees of respect, after a rotten apple tests the culture a few times—and believe me, they will—he or she will leave the environment in search of a culture they can contaminate.

In regards to who does what? Every stakeholder is involved. Everyone must honor and be excited to do the right thing because when it comes to issues of respect, you cannot have a written policy that addresses every single possibility. It is more a code of conduct than a list of rules.

SCOTT
I don't think there is a simple formula or process that works for every situation. That being said, the objective must be deliberate, modeled by leadership and clearly defined for all team members in writing: actions, individual objectives, and corporate goals. The proper behaviors when observed must be recognized, promoted, and celebrated. Accountability for inappropriate actions goes hand in hand. As far as who does what, leadership works to set, define, and communicate core values. Next, leaders must model the values, recognize and celebrate great examples of the values exhibited by employees

in the workplace. Doing this as a never-ending cycle will instill the behavior in the work culture. Once part of the culture, it will begin to emerge as an expected behavior from top down and bottom up.

MARIAN

This comes from the top down. Again, the top manager models respect and has to establish healthy, respectful work relationships. It begins in how they talk to their employees and address their concerns. This includes not entertaining gossip and keeping the employees focused and playing nice. The employees play a key role here too. Respect is shown in doing quality work, being a team player, and communicating well with each other and with management. When problems arise it is important for them to address it with their direct report, however do it in a respectful manner. This includes attitude and tone of delivery.

What are some of the unique challenges executives encounter in giving and receiving respect in the corporate structure?

JOHN

Executives must decipher what is truly respect and what is false respect from individuals who are just trying to manipulate you for their personal gain. In giving respect, you run the risk of hurting others' feelings. If I give a compliment to an employee, it gets amplified to others who hear it. You may give a compliment to one, but ten others will take it negatively. Jealousy, competition, and issues of ranking play into this. In the matter of disrespect, sometimes friends I have hired will goof off or poke fun at me in the work environment around other employees. In occasions like this, I've had to have crucial conversations to keep the work-friendship boundaries clear. In regards to receiving respect, some employees develop an attitude of ingratitude in the workplace. There is a sense of entitlement in the workplace today. For some, what you do for them appears to not be enough. There is a lack of appreciation, a "what have you done for me lately?" mentality. Some people are less respectful when you become successful. Instead, they become resentful.

SCOTT

Respect does not seem to be established in most homes and families today. The concept is foreign to many in the workplace. Establishing a new behavior in any individual once they've reached working age is challenging.

MARIAN

Just because you are an executive does not mean you will receive respect. However, an executive who treats his or her team with respect tends to also have it reciprocated. They also are likely to see higher motivation, morale, and productivity from their employees. Some executives operate from a position of power and control. They use manipulation to motivate their team. Unfortunately, this creates a culture of fear and mistrust. People are more inclined to watch their backs and shift blame than to actively move the corporate vision forward. In my experience with my team, when I set the tone by showing them respect, it always is reciprocated. Perhaps this is why some of them have worked for me for ten-plus years.

How does respect or the lack thereof effect morale and motivation at work?

JOHN

We lost key people due to a person who was disrespectful. If you set up the culture right, emphasizing respect, people will be harder on themselves to deliver for the team. However, if you allow disrespect to affect the culture, it will cost you. I lost a key employee because her manager was so rude and disrespectful to the team. Disrespect can destroy the whole culture. In my situation, I removed the manager. I don't think you can feel valued if you don't feel respected.

SCOTT

Most people desire, crave, and often demand respect. Without respect, they lack self-value and feel unappreciated by the company. This leads to poor morale, low productivity, and high turnover. However, sometimes individuals don't have any respect for themselves. In this case, it's very difficult to make them feel respected, no matter what you do.

MARIAN

As vice-president, it is my job to set the emotional tone in the workplace. If my morale is down because of a lack of support from upper-level executives my team can easily pick up on it. Therefore, it is important for me to work through these matters privately with my superiors so that it does not trickle down to my staff. Also, I have to keep up a positive attitude in times of adversity so they are not negatively influenced. In situations where I notice a morale problem within one or more members of my team, I take time to address the matter. In most cases, the morale issue can be resolved with a conversation that productively addresses the problem. Respectful communication is the key to maintaining healthy morale in the workplace.

When you have been shown respect how did you respond?

JOHN
After lively debate with senior management, as the CEO, I have made decisions that some senior team members did not agree with. With 360 degrees of respect, we all know we are each just trying to do the right thing for our stakeholders and whatever the decision outcome, we all carry it out as our own.

SCOTT
Each time I've been shown respect, it made me feel energized and happy. It also made me want to repeat the actions that led to the respect.

MARIAN
Overall, my staff treats me with respect. I appreciate it and reciprocate this behavior. As I said earlier, it is my responsibility to set the tone in the workplace. Respect is given after it has been received. I work among employees from various ranks and levels of income. When I walk into one of the corporate buildings in a major city and see an employee mopping the floor, I will greet him or her as warmly as I do a colleague or superior.

Were there times you have been shown disrespect? If so, how did you respond?

JOHN

Yes, I have experienced disrespect from time to time. My response obviously depends on the severity. I will say that humility is a tremendous asset in any situation of disrespect. Years ago, I had a COO that came into my office and started yelling at me. I collected myself and said, "Wait a minute." I then quietly said, "Let me ask a question. Imagine if you were shrunk down to about 6 inches tall and were perched up in the corner of my office and you were watching as the COO of the company came in the office of the CEO and began to yell at him. Now, what would you think of that COO?" Like a little boy that was just reprimanded by his father and realized what he did wrong, that Type A, alpha male slumped his shoulders, put his head down, and walked out of my office in embarrassment. That COO did not work out long term at our company. However, since moving on, he shared with me that I was one of the few people in his life that truly respected him. We are still friends today and we both have learned much from 360 degree respectful relationship.

SCOTT

Again, there have been many times. Each time, it made me feel angry and I was driven to change the circumstances that led to the disrespect. The actions to do this are as varied as the situations causing the lack of respect. This feels like a moving target due to the differing ways people feel and derive respect. There are eighteen hundred shades of the color white. You could pick any shade and be correct without picking the same shade that I prefer. Respect is probably as rich in variety.

MARIAN

One of the most disrespectful tactics is a fellow employee triangulating a problem with my superior. Rather than discussing a concern with me, maligning me to my boss is unprofessional and bad for a work environment. Individuals who do this not only lose my respect, but I find it difficult to trust them. To correct this problem, I talk directly with my boss about the triangulating pattern to prevent future occurrences.

Creating A Culture Of Respect In The Workplace

As you can see, respect in the workplace is key on multiple levels: employee morale, productivity and profit, customer satisfaction, and the vision and mission of the company. When disrespect permeates the work environment, it negatively impacts these areas, resulting in significant losses in people, productivity, and profit. Creating a culture of respect is a process that begins with those at the top: owners, presidents, executives, and managers. If you own your business, the process begins and ends with you.

I greatly admire another business leader, my friend Tony Orsini, president of Orsini Healthcare. Founded in 1987, Orsini Healthcare has become a leading provider in a growing home care industry. From one employee, the company grew with an entrepreneurial focus on in-home patient care, adding services and programs for more comprehensive home care solutions. Today, Orsini serves patients nationwide and has a commitment to develop an innovative organization with the people, programs, and technology that can achieve quality care. With a strong leadership team led by Orsini, the company remains grounded in the values that have guided its development and strengthened by a deep faith in the Christian mission to act justly, love mercy, and walk humbly with all those who have entrusted Orsini to care for their medical resources.

Tony has done an amazing job of changing the culture of his company over the past several years. Recently, I visited his company, was given a personal tour, met his employees, and sat down and talked with him about what he was doing to infuse respect in his work culture. Allow me to share some excerpts from my interview with Tony, which took place over several meetings.

DON

In your years as a business owner, what concerns you most in the workplace?

TONY

As a business leader I find myself resolving many problems in our company involving interpersonal relationships. It seems that there is a lack of EQ, emotional intelligence, in many individuals that work in companies today. I find it even more prevalent in the younger employees entering the work place.

DON

What do you do to address this problem?

TONY

At times, I feel like I must mentor our staff in the area of common respect and constructive communication. I find most people don't even understand their own communication style, core personality, fears, gifts, and strengths. We really need to establish a culture that not only encourages respect, but holds people accountable for lack of respect.

DON

What is your biggest problem with a lack of respect?

TONY

Our biggest problem with lack of respect is that it builds silos and turf wars between individuals and across departments. This creates an enormous drag on our productivity and cohesiveness as a company. When we have individuals and departments that are more concerned with their own agenda, we will never truly reach our potential as an organization. This lack of respect must be dealt with on a daily basis. It starts by having a clear mission that acknowledges how we are to act within the culture of our organization.

DON

Speaking of culture, I noticed in your work environment you have written core values. Could you talk about this?

TONY

We begin with steps that create an environment of clarity and accountability. Some of our core values are:

Transparency throughout the organization.

Speak the truth in love.

Crucial conversations, not critical confrontations.

Transformational leadership, not transactional leadership.

Development of EQ and self awareness throughout all levels of staff. If we can't discern how we communicate, are received by others, and how willing we are to hear others, we will never build healthy teams.

DON

What is your mission?

TONY

Our mission is to act justly, love mercy, and walk humbly. We also have a culture box that aligns all our decisions and behavior as an organization. One item in the culture box is respect. In addition, we value trust, transparency, and honesty, among others. As a company, we believe that in order for any of the staff to reach their true potential, we must help them to attain a level of health in 3 areas of their life: spiritual, physical, and emotional.

DON

Have you done anything to address these areas?

TONY

Yes. Recently, we hired a wellness director that works in developing an increased awareness of our staff in all three of these areas. We use four tests to help our employees develop better self-awareness. One is the Kiersey-Bates Temperament Sorter, which teaches individuals how they communicate and helps them understand how others receive this and how they respond. Once they are able to understand this difference, we notice an enormous improvement in respect and productivity.

The second test is the Enneagram in the work place personality test. This helps our staff to understand their core fears and the driving factors of their personality. Once they can understand how they view and respond to the world and workplace around them, they can also understand the hurdles that are in the way of developing a truly cohesive team. I have learned that when we understand ourselves and others, we can create a platform of respect for each other and our adapt around our differences. This has had an enormous difference in helping us tear down the silos and stop turf wars that raged on in our company. We now have a common platform to understand each other.

The third test is the Strength Finders. It helps us identify each individual's gifts and help them embrace these strengths. When we can help them move toward embracing and utilizing these gifts we as an organization will begin to truly benefit.

The fourth is a physical fitness assessment and health plan.

DON

How has this additional training in the area of emotional intelligence changed your work culture?

TONY

We have seen enormous increase in productivity and connectedness within our teams. As we have developed common shared values, an environment of serving as well as doing life together has emerged. We have made significant improvement in showing respect for each other. From a spiritual standpoint, we created enormous serving opportunities for our entire workforce. For example, we conduct regular trips to Nicaragua to help those living in extreme poverty to get their basic survival needs met. A typical trip would feature a team comprising employees in all departments: warehouse, drivers, accounts receivable, customer service, and senior leadership working together, serving in an orphanage. As we serve side-by-side, we develop a greater respect for each other and the talents we bring to bear in service to the disadvantaged. We have found that cross-training individuals even for as little as a few hours in other departments has created a much greater degree of respect and team spirit. When they walk a mile or so in each other's shoes, they come out of the experience with a whole new perspective.

DON

Any final thoughts about respect in the workplace that might help other business owners?

TONY

A very important aspect of developing respect is working very hard to assure that cascading messages are being communicated from senior leadership throughout every corner of the organization. Now more then ever, we as business leaders need to model respect to every level of our organization. We need to be very vigilant in assuring that our culture is not hijacked by a leader with their own agenda. We had a leader begin to lead in a culture of absolute disrespect toward those whom he deemed as nonessential level staff members. This action created a hostile and abusive environment, which took down an entire department. We needed to act immediately upon finding this out. The willingness to establish a clear culture box and engage with all levels of staff who violate this culture is a significant challenge for many leaders. When we have a high-level producer who consistently violates our policy of respect, it takes a high-level commitment from the CEO and president to take decisive action. A culture of respect must come first.

What You Can Do To Bring Respect Back In The Workplace

Respect in the workplace can mean different things, depending on your role within your company or organization. Similar to a family, hierarchy plays a role here. Employers expect their employees to respect the company. Employees have expectations about respect from their employers and coworkers. People in managerial positions like Kevin also seek respect from upper management in addition to those they supervise.

Think about your role in your workplace. Whether you are at the top, bottom, or sandwiched in-between, you *invest* in or *infect* the company by the respect you give or fail to show to others. As we heard from those interviewed, disrespect is a threat not only to a company's success, but also to the job security of those who spread it in the workplace. You could be out of a job if you do not respect the company and its employees. Before I close this chapter on respect in the workplace, let me offer some things to think about.

Suggestions for Business Owners

If you are a business owner, you set the tone for your organization. A culture of respect begins and ends with you. You must model respect in the way you interact with your employees, in all levels of your organizational chart. Do you spend all your time with upper level management? How often do you interact with lower-level employees? To better understand business operations and to get to know his employees better, Tony Orsini temporarily moved out of his corner office and found a cubicle among his employees. Every day, he met with one of his employees for a cup of coffee and a conversation about their personal lives and their perspective on business operations. He related to me that this was one of the most powerful and meaningful experiences he has had in his career as CEO. Not only did it help the company recover hundreds of thousands of dollars of uncollected receivables, but he used what he learned to train his managers to become better leaders of their teams.

I make it a practice to show manners and be respectful wherever I go. For example, I use titles Sir or Ma'am when I receive service in a restaurant, store, or when someone offers a simple service, such as a bus boy pouring me a glass of water. While I do this out of basic respect for people, I notice that these individuals will elevate their level of service in response. As I have stated throughout this book, respect is reciprocal. Apply this to the workplace and you will find for the most part, people to whom you show respect will return it by working hard, being a team player, and having a good attitude at work.

Suggestions for Managers

Creating a culture of respect is challenging when your superiors do not set the tone. Consequently, you may be experiencing disrespect from above and below. You can probably relate to the frustrations Kevin emoted. While challenging, it is not impossible to create a culture of respect in your work domain. You can set the tone for your team by showing respect to everyone who works for you. Change will begin with how you act toward them.

I recommend you begin meeting one-on-one with your team. Spend a little time getting to know them. Ask for their input on how the department could run more efficiently. Where you notice potential areas of improvement in terms of job performance and social interaction, discuss these areas with them. If possible, offer training to help them improve their social awareness and communication skills.

One of the keys to establishing and maintaining respect in the work culture that was discussed in the interviews above concerns taking action when you see a pattern of disrespect with one or more employees. As a leader and manager, you do not want others to undermine your authority and corrupt the work environment with poisonous behavior. Employees will look to you to intervene and put an end to it. If you don't, the morale will suffer and good people may leave the company. Address the problem correctly, keeping in mind the policies outlined in your human resources manual.

If you think you could improve upon your leadership skills in the area of emotional intelligence, I suggest you consider working with an executive coach. Investment in executive coaching can help you add new skills, while sharpening current ones. The training aspect of executive coaching will assist you in practicing new skills. In addition, you can learn how to address current problems with proven solutions, which will elevate your standing among your peers. Executive coaching is becoming increasingly popular among managers and leaders of companies.

Suggestions for Employees

Have you heard the biblical adage,[8] *"Bad company corrupts good character"*? If you associate with employees who gossip or bad-mouth other employees, managers, or ownership, they can infect your attitude negatively. On the other hand, if you choose to show respect to others in your company, you will enjoy your work, have more energy, be efficient with your time, and you will likely find favor with your superiors.

If you have a problem with a fellow employee, try to work it out between the two of you. If the other person is unwilling, then you may seek conflict resolution support from your manager. Perhaps you can request a transfer to another department. If a problem with respect arises with your boss or manager, ask for a meeting and discuss your concerns with him or her. Also, be open to feedback on how you may be contributing to the problem. Seek solutions that will prevent the problem from occurring again between the two of you. If you are proactive, with a modicum of respect, it is likely the matter will be resolved and the relationships strengthened.

Finally, if you want to develop the qualities of respect, emotional intelligence, and good work ethic, I suggest you find a mentor who can help you develop these traits. A mentor can be anyone you know who exhibits these qualities. They don't have to be a business owner or manager, although this would be helpful if you aspire along this path. A mentor is a person who has worked faithfully, performed their duties with

---

8   The Holy Bible - Book of 1Corinthians 15:33

excellence, was dependable, and known by others for their character and the respect they show to others. A mentor can meet with you on an informal basis, over a cup of coffee. The purpose is for the mentor to pour into your life and help you understand how you can handle the adult responsibilities of a worker.

An entire book can be devoted to the topic of respect in the workplace. My hope is this chapter has inspired you to join a revolution of respect. Let's shift from work to an even bigger task—bringing respect back into society. Our chapter begins with Brandon trying to enforce some respect in his school and ends with the story of a boy and a starfish.

Chapter Eight

Bringing Respect Back In Society

Kevin is punching away at the keyboard working feverishly to get a report done for the department meeting set for 3:00pm. As long he's not interrupted, he can get this project done in time. He glances at the clock and hammers away at the keys. Suddenly, his cell phone vibrates and he notices it is Brandon's school. *This can't be good*, he whispers to himself. Kevin hits the call button and braces for what he is about to hear.

"Your son has been in a fight and is being suspended from school. We need you to come and pick him up now."

The dean tells him how Brandon punched a student in the mouth, resulting in a lacerated lip that will require stitches. Kevin assures the dean he will leave work immediately to escort his son from school. Thinking about the pile of work on his desk and the department meeting in one hour, Kevin is rattled, to say the least.

A year ago, Kevin would not be the person dealing with this problem. Heidi would have been the person the school called. Now that he has been stepping up in his role as dad, Kevin has agreed to have his phone number on the top of the list to call. After he informs his boss of an emergency, he jumps in his car and calls Heidi from the road.

"Brandon's been in a fight at school and I'm on the way to pick him up. He is being suspended. I don't know all the details, but I'll fill you in later."

Heidi says, "I'll meet you at the school."

"Never mind," says Kevin. "No sense in both of us leaving work. I'll handle it. Thanks for offering."

Heidi responds, "You okay?"

Kevin answers, "I'm angry that he hit someone, but also confused. I'm not jumping to conclusions. I want to get to the bottom of this. My emotions are under control for now. I can handle it."

Kevin arrives in the dean's office where he finds Brandon slumped in a chair with an angry scowl on his face. The dean informs Kevin that Brandon is being suspended from school until further notice, pending an investigation of the incident by individuals who witnessed what happened. Kevin escorts Brandon from the school without a word muttered by either of them.

Once they get into the car and pull out of the driveway, Kevin calmly asks Brandon, "What led you to punch the student?"

With his back toward his dad and facing toward the passenger window, Brandon responds, "I don't want to talk about it. It's stupid. If they want to suspend me, go ahead. I'd do it again!"

Confused, Kevin responds, "You'd punch someone in the face? What for, Brandon? Why'd you do it in the first place?"

Brandon turns toward his dad and screams, "Because they deserved it. This idiot Marcus and his friend were taunting Jared, calling him a fag because he's gay."

In a calming manner, Kevin replies, "Oh, I see. So you were defending someone being bullied. Why'd you decide to hit this bully?"

Kevin listens as Brandon recounts what happened in the hallway between classes. Brandon tells him how these two students were teasing Jared to the point he was in tears. They started making crude gestures and knocked his books on the floor. When Brandon told them to knock it off, Marcus said, "Who are you, his gay lover?" In response, Brandon clocked him in the eye.

Brandon continues. "Next thing I know, a teacher comes running up and marches me to the dean. Because I was the only person who threw a punch, I'm suspended. Jared tried to explain what happened, that I was defending him, but whatever. They're saying I'm to blame for the hit."

Kevin pulls the car over in a nearby parking lot, turns off the ignition, and looks Brandon in the eye. "Wow, Son. I have mixed feelings here. I'm proud of you for defending Jared. It was awful what those boys did to him. You came to his aid by confronting their bullying. I'm a little disappointed that you lost your cool and hit Marcus. Do you think there was another way to handle the situation?"

Brandon responded, "Yeah, I could have ignored the comment and walked away with Jared, but to be honest, I don't think it would have stopped him. Marcus would keep doing it. This taunting has been going on for a while and I'm sick of it. The jerk had it coming to him. He deserved what he got."

Kevin offers Brandon something to think about. "I get it. Mission accomplished. You put an end to the bullying. They'll think twice about making fun of Jared. However, ask yourself this question. "Did I deserve to be punished in the end?" You're right, walking away would not have solved the problem. Walking to a teacher or the dean and informing them of what you witnessed would. Bullying is against school policy. Perhaps these boys would be the ones suspended if you told the authorities, rather than take the matter in your own hands. Something to think about next time. Now I have one final thing to say. I'm proud of you for standing up for Jared."

"Well, thanks. I suppose I'm now grounded for being suspended, right?"

"Let me discuss this with Mom and we'll decide if another punishment is warranted here. I'm more interested in what you learn from this experience. What concerns me most is how you'll handle a situation like this in the future. Can you stand for what you believe in while controlling your emotions?"

Brandon ponders for a moment. "The way you handled this situation with me kind of teaches me how to handle things in the future."

"What do you mean?"

"Well, I thought you would come to school screaming at me for doing something stupid, getting suspended, and interrupting your day at work. But you were actually calm and asked me to tell you what happened. When you're calm, I listen to what you're trying to get me to understand. Maybe I'll try your approach next time. Thanks for not losing control dad."

Bringing Respect Back Begins At Home

As you can see by the manner in which the Hughes family navigated their way through this recent crisis, they have come a long way in building respectful relationships. Kevin and Heidi are partners in parenting, and Brandon is allowing his dad to be a dad. Old patterns are giving way to new ones and the result is less family anxiety and more quality connection. Together, they have successfully created a culture of respect in the home.

Interestingly, the value of respect is also seeping into their social worlds. Take Brandon for example. Disinterested in school and not much of a social person, limiting his circle to a few close friends, he garnishes much attention by defending a gay student on campus. His motive was not to cause trouble or get negative attention. Rather, it was to teach his peers to be respectful of people who are different. While his method got him into trouble, it should not overshadow the fact that he was an advocate for social respect. I suspect Brandon was practicing in his social life what he was learning at home.

Bringing respect back in society begins at home. As I discussed in previous chapters, we learn our social behavior by what is taught and caught at home. By teaching, modeling, and reinforcing respect, it becomes a trait that governs social behavior. The Hughes family shows us it's never too late to establish respect in the home. It may begin with one person making the decision and it can spread throughout the family. More often than not, when we show respect, most people will reciprocate. It may take a little longer to generate it in the family, but if you keep at it, the pattern will emerge.

As I discussed in the beginning of the book, respect has somehow lost its standing as a preeminent value governing social behavior in our society. I suppose we can go back to the founding of our country and see torrid examples of disrespect shown to Native Americans, people of color, and women who were treated in horrific manner by individuals who justified their actions under the guise of patriotism, religion, or manifest destiny. Throughout American history, we have struggled to get it right. While we made some progress in leveling the playing field in areas such as civil rights, we still have a problem getting along.

As I write this chapter, several news stories are making headlines. Jerry Sandusky, a former assistant football coach at Penn State University was found guilty of forty-five counts of criminal sexual assault of a minor. This is a scandal that allegedly includes a cover-up by university personnel who chose to protect the university's interests over the welfare of minor boys preyed upon by Sandusky in the charity program he established.

Another example involved a sixty-eight year-old woman named Karen Klein, who served as a bus monitor for a junior high school in upstate New York. A video camera caught four seventh grade boys taunting her mercilessly with profanity, insults, and threats while she was doing her best to ignore them. At one point, a student who knew the bus monitor's oldest son had committed suicide ten years ago said, "You don't have a family because they all killed themselves because they don't want to be near you." The video shows Ms. Klein breaking down in tears.

Public outcry over this video has been widespread. Money has poured in well into the six-figure level as an expression of support for Ms. Klein. True to the American spirit, when we see someone who has been traumatized, we rush in to provide relief, usually in the form of financial support. However, throwing money at the problem won't cure the underlying symptom. Nor will a financial settlement from Penn State heal the emotional scars these young men will live with the rest of their lives. What does it say about our culture that we choose not to protect innocent children and the elderly?

I can devote another hundred pages to examples of disrespect shown to people based on their religious beliefs, ethnicity, sexual orientation, disability, political views, or socioeconomic status. It appears every segment of society is fair game to insults, threats, and other forms of disrespect. The purpose here is not to rant about the problem but to appeal to my fellow citizens to join me in bringing respect back to society. It begins first with bringing self-respect back and follows with showing every person we meet some basic respect.

You may be thinking I have some John Lennon notion of "Imagine" going on here. I'm not clamoring for utopia. If I can show respect to one person, what will it mean in that moment, or the individual's day for that matter? Can I put a smile on the person's face, help them feel a little self-respect? I know when I am shown respect in a store, I am very likely to be a returning customer. They may be trained to act that way, but it works! Innate within us all is the need to be accepted and shown respect. When this happens, it draws us to people, not away.

Want to influence people? Want to influence culture? Show some respect—simple as that. So how do we do this in a diverse culture? Here are some suggestions.

Use A Single Lens Of Respect

Influencing change requires having a single lens of respect for all people. Instinctively, many of us change lenses when viewing people from different backgrounds. The lens may have a higher degree of suspicion, mistrust, or prejudice toward others who don't share our backgrounds. Our favorite glasses to wear have matching lenses with other people. We like our glasses to match our friends. In other words, we prefer hanging with others who are just like us. We tend to gravitate to people who share our skin color, beliefs, political views, social interests, and so on. It's less complicated to navigate our social world when we hang with people who see the world the way we do.

However, when we are with people who are different, we sometimes change the lens and formulate opinions and judgments based on these differences. We rank people based on our views of what is acceptable or not. These attitudes govern our social interactions and lead to misassumptions and miscommunication, costing us opportunities to know people from different walks of life and to find common ground.

Throughout human history, we have struggled with diversity. However, in some places, we find people who break these barriers by seeing everyone through a single lens of respect. The church I attend is culturally diverse. In fact, my wife and I—both Caucasian, born in the United States—are minorities in the demographics of the church. This morning, the communion service was led by our pastor a Ukrainian immigrant, his assistant pastor who was an African immigrant, and two lay leaders, one African American and the other a Hispanic American. For me, it was a snapshot of heaven.

How can people of such diverse backgrounds come together around the table of communion? Well, several reasons come to mind, in particular our common faith in Jesus Christ. Also, there is an unconditional acceptance of cultural differences and our commonality as children of

God. While we come from different backgrounds, we respect each other's right to be who we are and express ourselves in a manner that reflects our individuality. It is expressed in our language, dress, mannerisms, and even our food.

The campus where I teach is a beautiful cross-section of racial, ethnic, religious, and socioeconomic diversity blended in a setting where we are all equal and striving together to reach our academic goals. This environment breaks down barriers and requires students to interact in a manner that allows them to get to know one another on their academic journey. Here, we deal with the problems of prejudice, inequality, and disrespect. We learn by listening to one another's stories and find we have more in common than we thought. It's interesting how your view of things changes when you invest time with people different from you.

Recently, I had to renew my driver's license and was required to have a vision test. To my surprise, I passed in the right eye and failed in the left. A couple of weeks later, I was tested by an ophthalmologist who discovered I have a problem with the cells in the back of my cornea that regulate moisture. My cells are few and dying rapidly. Restoring my vision requires a partial cornea transplant. My left eye is worse than my right, so the stronger eye has been compensating for the weaker. I didn't realize my vision was distorted until I took the test.

I think our society suffers from disrespect dystrophy. Many of us are plagued with conditions of prejudice and are not aware because we compensate for it with an ethnocentric lens. In other words, we think the world should operate from our point of view. Consequently, we shake our heads in confusion when people don't see things as obviously as we do. Yet we live in a world of such diversity. What keeps us from seeing the world through a single lens of respect?

Ignorance and fear are conditions that distort our field of vision. This causes us to act in a disrespectful manner toward one another. Ignorance happens when we don't seek to understand others and draw conclusions about them from afar. Fear creates space between people of diversity who feel threatened that others may try to change or control them. Choosing a single lens of respect corrects the distortion caused by ignorance and fear.

Respect draws us toward people, not away from them. Try it for yourself. Using a single lens of respect, why not make an effort today to connect with someone who is different from you. It might be a person from a different religion, skin color, sexual orientation, socioeconomic background or political view. Be friendly, smile, and extend a warm greeting. This will help you correct the distortion caused by ignorance and fear.

Develop The Art Of Curiosity

Curiosity, paired with good listening skills, is an effective means of showing others respect. Recently I wrote an article, *"Curiosity, the Cure for Confusing Communication."* In it, I talked about how taking an interest in what others think and feel, opens the channels of communication and creates understanding between people. The curiosity I'm referring to is not *interrogative* but *inquisitive*, much like an innocent child investigating something for the first time. It's about learning, discovering, and integrating an understanding of something new, something different. It doesn't mean you have to agree with everything you hear, but it does mean you should consider it—and most importantly—respect it.

As an educator in counseling, I teach graduate students that the single-most effective intervention in clinical practice is the skill of curiosity. It is easy for professionals to quickly diagnose problems based on the familiarity of our clinical work. Personally, every individual is unique and fascinating. I listen closely to their stories and I am curious about how they see the world and view their problems. Treatment plans are collaborated through a series of curious questions in my attempt to see the world through their eyes. Though the problems I treat are familiar, the individuals nonetheless are unique and their experiences quite personal. My curiosity in them and their stories is showing them respect and serves to solidify the bond we form so the work can be accomplished in a caring manner.

Think about an individual or particular cultural group for whom you have formed a bias based upon ignorance or fear. What might you do to correct this distorted view? Would you consider getting to know them? What are some non-threatening, curious questions you might ask to begin a friendly dialog? You see how simple it is? Begin with an acquaintance. It could be a fellow employee, a neighbor, or someone who works in the grocery store or the café you frequent.

It's not too big a challenge to get acquainted with people who are culturally different. How about taking the plunge to get to know someone with whom you don't agree? For those who've developed a biases about others from afar, I offer you a challenge. Liberal, why not have some hang time with a conservative? Atheist with a believer in God. Straight with gay. I'm not asking you to argue your views with each other, win a convert, or destroy an opponent. Simply spend time getting to know them as a person apart from their orientation. If you choose to discuss your differences, take a position of curiosity first. Try to understand them before you offer your views.

I think St. Francis of Assisi got the sequence right when he prayed, *"O Divine Master, grant that I may not so much seek to be consoled as to console, to be understood, as to understand, to be loved, as to love..."* In the end, you may continue to see the world differently, but you are likely to have a greater understanding and respect of each other. Perhaps a friendship may develop. You'd be surprised what happens when ignorance, fear, and prejudice no longer distort your views—when respect, acceptance, and friendship emerge.

Replace Hypocrisy With Some Humility

We are a society that likes to rant about what we don't like and build ourselves up by putting others down. Technology provides many portals for people to express their views about what is happening in our country. I am all for freedom of speech and I enjoy reading and dialoging over topics in politics, sports, or other issues of the day. What troubles me is how individuals can express their views in such a rude and inconsiderate manner, using expletives, ethnic and racial slurs, or other forms of disrespectful language.

The blame game is rampant in our society. Politicians blame the other party; it's a rarity when someone takes ownership. Why does everything have to be someone else's fault? Sometimes I will watch talk shows that feature representatives from opposing political views talking about important issues. It's like watching a sibling argument in front of parents. The commentators interrupt each other, yell, and blame each other, while no one is really answering the questions. Perhaps this is done to boost ratings. If so, what does it say about the intelligence of the average citizen? We don't want solid, undiluted journalism? All we aspire to is entertainment? I don't think so!

Pointing fingers is not solely a political tactic; it can be observed in all social institutions. When kids act out in school through acts of bullying, violence, or other socially inappropriate ways, fingers point in all directions. Schools blame parents and parents blame schools. Media and the entertainment industry are also indicted for encouraging kids to act out. Rarely do we see individuals stand before society, take ownership, and admit they are wrong. A little humility with some basic honesty would do us all some good.

As you can tell by now, spirituality is an important aspect of my life. My Christian faith is the core of my identity. One of the things I have learned along my spiritual journey is the reality that I am imperfect. I also know that when I confess my weaknesses, I find strength in God to overcome them. Humility plays a huge role in how I connect with God, myself, and others. In other words, I have a more accurate view of life when I embrace the idea that we are all broken people needing help from God to make the best of our days on earth.

Please allow me a moment to speak about a problem I observe in my church community. I am embarrassed to admit that within the Christian church, humility often gives way to hypocrisy. While the role of the Church in society is to represent the law of God, the manner in which this is done is not always Christlike. At times, we give off an air of superiority and act judgmental toward those with whom we disagree. Church leaders speak out against the sins of society, yet are found to be guilty of similar acts of greed, sexual misconduct, or other forms of fraudulent behavior. We have been mandated by Christ to be "the light of the world...the salt of the earth," but when we act in a hypocritical manner, we lose our influence in society.

Recently, I was in a conversation with several Christian leaders about a particular controversial issue in society. Someone asked, "Would you attend a wedding ceremony of a relative if it was a gay marriage?"

As opinions were vented in the room, I asked the question, "What would Jesus do if he were here today?"

One of the participants responded how Jesus took a stand on issues by "turning over tables."

My response was, "He did that in the *Temple*."

Later that day, as I thought more about our discussion, the image of tables and Jesus entered my mind. As I reflected, it came to me that Jesus flipped tables in the Temple and reclined at tables in the homes of sinners. In the Temple, he was angry that the religious leaders in their hypocrisy were taking advantage of people who came to worship God by exploiting them. The stand he took was against hypocrisy in a religious setting. However, when reclined in the homes of tax collectors, prostitutes, and others who were considered socially degenerate people, he accepted them where they were without casting judgment on them. He focused on sharing with them the unconditional love of God that could fill the void in their lives and free them from bondage.

For example, there is a story about when Jesus went to a well. A woman there asked if she could pour him some water. He in turn offered her "living water." Over the course of the conversation, he told her he was aware of her past marital history—six failed marriages—and that she was currently living with a man who wasn't her husband. He didn't say, "Straighten out your life and come back and see me." Rather, he offered her something to quench her soul, something that could fill the void in her life in a way that men could not. His actions with her were not intended to condemn nor condone her behavior, but to offer her something better.

He took a similar approach with the woman who was caught in adultery and brought to him by the religious leaders. They wanted her to be stoned based on Jewish law.

Jesus' response to the leaders was, "You who are without sin, cast the first stone." Here, he addressed their hypocrisy. They all walked away. To the woman he said, "Where are your accusers?"

She replied, "They are gone."

Jesus said to her, "Neither do I accuse you. Go, and sin no more."

He who was without sin could have stoned her, but he showed her mercy and instructed her to change her ways.

Notice how Jesus treated both women with respect? I think this is what he is trying to teach those of us in the Christian faith. We have to stop being judgmental and hypocritical and show humility to others. No one is perfect. Judgment is God's business, not ours. Instead, we would be served well to walk in Jesus' shoes. He did not suspend his views on spirituality or morality. He met people where they were, getting to know them, allowing them to know him. Through relationship with others, he was able to show them the path of life.

The notion of superiority is a huge barrier to respect. It is a danger to our society. If I think I outrank you because of my bank account, skin color, gender, religion, or other factor, the perceived power imbalance will cause problems. However, if we base respect simply on our shared humanity, then we all have equal footing. This is why I propose we show more humility and knock off the hypocrisy. We are imperfect people living in an imperfect world. Let's use a single lens of respect for all people and we can get our society back on track.

Show Tolerance While Holding To Your Values

Tolerance is a buzz word in the multiculturalism and diversity movement. Essentially, it refers to the right of existence for all people, including the freedom to express oneself without judgment or punitive outcomes. One of the arguments I often hear discussed around this issue is an expectation that tolerance is meant to be synonymous with agreement. In other words, if I am to show tolerance, I must modify my ideology to include the views of others. If this is the expectation, then tolerance cannot be reciprocal. Mutual tolerance suggests that people extend to each other the right of self-expression within the laws of the land.

In a pluralistic society, we allow everyone the inalienable right of self-expression. Consider again the intent of the Declaration of Independence: *"We hold these truths to be self-evident, that all men are created equal, that they are endowed by the Creator with certain unalienable Rights, that among these are Life, Liberty and the pursuit of Happiness."* Government's job is to protect these rights for the people. Over the course of history, we have fought hard battles from without and within to ensure these rights to our citizens. Currently, we face a new type of war, a battle for cultural supremacy.

Postmodernism promotes the idea that truth is subjective, not absolute. This shift in thinking creates tension in a society whose foundation is based on fundamental principles and theocratic underpinnings. Thus, within our pluralistic society are proponents for liberalism matched against champions for conservatism. In between these polarities are moderates, libertarians, and other, smaller sociopolitical groups.

A struggle continues over the direction our society will take, with both sides of the cultural divide fighting for control. This battle is fierce and at times ugly, with covert activities on both sides intended to malign the other in an attempt to silence their right to speak. Apparently, when the stakes are high, individuals will resort to unscrupulous tactics to push their agenda. This strategy is certainly does not demonstrate respect for an opponent, nor does it fare well with the general public.

Perhaps we can achieve tolerance on a macro-level when we demonstrate it on a micro-level, where an individual exhibits respect toward another with whom he or she shares opposing views. Discussion or debate is a healthy exercise when done with more than a modicum of respect. The sharing of power in this exchange allows influence to flow.

With mutual respect, both individuals are given the right to express their thoughts and feelings about issues that are important to them. They achieve understanding of perspectives and reach outcomes without damaging the integrity of the relationship. In some instances, individuals may amend their views, at other times they may agree to disagree. However, in both situations, individuals do not allow their opposing views to interfere in their personal relationship.

One of my favorite writers who has stirred my thinking about respect is Martin Buber, a Jewish theologian who wrote the book *I and Thou*. He talks about the importance of knowing yourself and knowing others. Buber addresses the importance of not losing a sense of yourself in an attempt to know and get along with others. In talking about this balance, Buber said, *"It takes a lifetime to learn how to be able to hold your own ground, to go out to others, to be open to them without losing your ground, and to hold your ground without shutting others out."*

For me, Buber captures the essence of tolerance. It allows opposing views to coexist not at the expense of personal beliefs or interpersonal relationships. I may not see the world as you do, but we can respect each other's right to live in it, and when our paths intersect, we will yield each other the right of way.

Find Common Ground To Stand On

There are occasions when ideologies are set aside for a common purpose. One such time was September 11, 2001, when terrorists assaulted our country. Once the imminent threat to national security was ensured, politicians put their differences aside and joined on the steps of the Capitol in a show of unity to stand with our President and defend our country. Here, common ground was the threat to our national security from without. We often reach common ground when we face a mutual threat to freedom or security.

It reminds me of a story a tour guide told at an arboretum where my wife and I are members. He was talking about how controlled burns in the prairies are conducted to promote a healthy ecology. On one occasion, as the fire was burning the prairie grass, a fox and a rabbit were observed simultaneously running for safety. Much to his surprise, they ran for cover into the same hole. Later, when the danger of fire subsided, the two animals emerged from the hole and ran in opposite directions. In a time of mutual danger, they huddled together in a foxhole not as adversaries, but as co-survivors.

Common ground can be found not only when it comes to security or freedom, but also where mutual interests are concerned. For divorced parents, that may be the children. Coming together in a respectful manner to co-parent is essential to the welfare of the children. This requires adults putting their differences aside when it comes to doing what is in the best interests of the kids. On a fundamental level, ex-spouses must never pit their children against the other parent in a battle for control. Instead, parents must grant each other equal access to the children and encourage the relationship.

Finding common ground in families is not always easy. Relationships are often ruptured by opposing political views, religious beliefs, or matters of sexual orientation. For some, as I stated earlier, tolerance is akin to agreement and their family relationships suffer. What's lacking in these decisions is acceptance. Accepting people for who they are does not mean you always have to agree with what they do. The common ground may not be your beliefs, but your biology, your familial roots. Don't allow your principles to separate you from the people you love. If you reject someone because you don't agree with them, the relationship may suffer lasting consequences. Instead, find common ground so that your principles and the people you love can coexist in your world.

Bringing Respect Full-Circle

Brandon waited to hear what his parents decided would be his consequences for punching the student at school. After dinner, his parents sat down and revisited the incident with him. They asked Brandon if he learned something from the situation and what he thought his punishment should be. Brandon answered, "I learned that punching that kid was a stupid thing to do. I let him get to me and I lost control. Hurting Marcus was no different from what he did to Jared. We were both bullies."

Kevin and Heidi looked at each other and nodded, signaling they approved of his response.

"What about your punishment?" Kevin asked.

Here, Brandon really got their attention. "I guess I should be grounded or something like that. But to tell you the truth, I have been feeling really bad about hitting that kid. If I were to give myself a punishment, I guess it would be to apologize for hitting him."

Astonished, Heidi said, "You just gave yourself the consequence we planned to give you. How did you come to this decision on your own?"

"You and Dad have been making a big deal out of showing respect at home. It's made things go better with all of us. I wanted Jared to be shown respect, but I realized when I punched Marcus that I acted like I used to at home. In the past, it wouldn't have bothered me. It's weird, but now it does. I have to make it right or I won't feel better about myself."

Brandon followed through on his self-prescribed punishment and apologized to the student he punched. When the school conducted their investigation, they discovered how Jared was being bullied. Upon further investigation, they also learned that Brandon apologized Marcus.

The students involved were brought together with the school socialworker and the dean to talk about the incident in a series of meetings that allowed repairs to be made and relationships to be forged based on mutual respect. This group held an assembly and talked with their peers about the lessons they learned and a campaign they planned to lead that would abolish bullying and promote respect among students. The student body embraced the idea and it had a positive affect on the social climate of the school.

Have you alienated people in your world by the way in which you have chosen to take a stand on an issue? Maybe you haven't wounded others using physical force, but have you lashed out with your words or punished them with emotional distance? Marcus called Jared a fag because he was gay. This was unkind and hurtful. Condemning someone to hell because they are gay is judgmental and devoid of the unconditional love of God. Using ethnic or racial slurs is also disrespectful.

Bringing respect back to society may begin with repairing some wounds with people you have hurt. It may be a coworker, neighbor, family member, or friend you have alienated. I recommend you go to the person and attempt to repair the relationship. Perhaps you are both wrong, but someone has to start to make it right. Why not you?

One of the most shameful days of my life occurred as a teenager when a few of my friends drove into an African-American neighborhood on the border of our neighborhood on the south-side of Chicago. As a teenager was riding his bike, we pulled alongside of him and I hit him in the back with a wooden stick. He fell over off his bike and got up again and started riding after our car. While we sped away, my friends laughed and applauded my behavior. Smiling on the outside, I cringed on the inside with intense feelings of guilt and shame.

I remember a few years earlier, when the community I had lived in as a boy transitioned from all white to predominantly black. We were one of the last white families in the community. My best friends were black. It was the time of the Civil Rights Movement and Dr. Martin Luther-King had been assassinated.

Suddenly, my neighborhood was not safe. Several times over the course of the next few years, my siblings and I were attacked by angry African-American youth. As a boy, I didn't understand why we had been bullied unjustly. Later, as a teen, provoked by my friends, I struck back. It did not make me feel better. I felt horrible. The boy on the bike was no different from me a few years earlier. I vowed after that incident that I would never use my hurt to hurt back.

Bringing respect back to society happens one person at a time.

Recently, my wife and I spent a few days in San Francisco, a combination of business and pleasure. Having travelled here several times I have developed a fondness for the city on the bay and all that it offers. It is a melting pot of cultural diversity, beauty, history, and amazing restaurants!

While my wife was attending a seminar, I did some writing on this project. We made reservations for dinner at a new, popular restaurant and decided to walk there which was about a mile away. Navigating the streets of downtown San Francisco during evening rush hour is no easy task. The sidewalks were jammed with people in a hurry to get wherever they needed to go.

As we were walking around a busy corner, I accidentally brushed alongside a young woman who was going in the opposite direction. I turned and politely said, "I'm sorry ma'am." Simultaneously, she twirled around, flicked her cigarette at me, hitting me in the arm, and shouted an obscenity while giving me the middle finger. Then she quickly turned away and continued walking. My wife and I looked at each other with stunned expressions.

It may sound weird, but when the incident occurred, her movements seemed to go in slow motion: the flicking of the cigarette, watching it hit my arm and fall to the ground, looking back at her and seeing the woman standing there defiantly with an angry scowl on her face. My initial reaction was feeling assaulted, followed by a fight-flight response. However, I experienced no anger or fear in my reaction. As I looked back at the woman I felt sorry for her.

As we continued our walk to the restaurant we talked about the incident. I said to my wife, "She seems like she carries a lot of anger inside her. I imagine underneath the anger is hurt. Let's remember to pray for her later." When we returned to our hotel and settled in to bed, we did pray for the woman. Actually, whenever I think about the incident I pray she finds peace in her soul. Of course, this woman has no idea how I interpreted the incident or her behavior for that matter. Perhaps she thought I was rude for invading her space and labels me a jerk. While I consider her actions toward me disrespectful, I chose not to reciprocate in like manner.

Did it matter to the woman that I did not retaliate? Probably not. My impression of her is that she is always ready for a fight. I don't think she felt ashamed or guilty for her actions. She may have felt some vindication. In the end, my behavior is what matters to me. I chose to be respectful toward her when the incident occurred and will continue to do so when her image crosses my mind. Maybe one day my prayers for her will make a difference in her life. I happen to believe they will.

For every person who reacts rudely to a respectful gesture, there are many more who will show appreciation. The truth is, the vast majority of us want to be shown respect. When respect is conveyed it says, "You matter". It reminds me of a story about a boy and a starfish.

A boy was found throwing starfish back into the ocean amidst a multitude laying on the shore. A man watched him tossing one starfish after another back into the water, barely making a dent in the mass that were littered on the sand.

The man approached him and asked, "With so many starfish on the shore, do you think what you are doing matters?"

As he tossed the next starfish into the ocean, the boy responded, "It matters to this one."

At that, the man joined the boy in saving starfish.

I suppose if one person takes on the challenge of showing respect, I will have another person joining me on the shore. The respect you show to someone else may not change the world, but it will matter to the person who is on the receiving end. Think about the impact you can have on one person when you bring respect back into your relationships. Kevin's respect toward Brandon had an impact on him. He was able to bring respect into his social world. Care to join me on the shore?

Chapter Nine

When Respect Doesn't Happen

Heidi's phone rings. Instantly, she feels nausea. The ringtone, "Hotel California," is assigned to the one person she dreads talking to the most—her mother. For Heidi, this is the one relationship she feels like, *"…you can check out any time you want / but you can never leave."* Heidi feels trapped in a toxic relationship with her mom. She clutches the phone while pacing the floor.

> KEVIN
> Heidi, do not answer the phone. You know what's she going to do.
> HEIDI
> Yeah, but if I don't talk to her, she'll make me pay.
> KEVIN
> You're getting punished either way. So she gives you the silent treatment. It's better than letting her shred you with criticism then heap on the guilt.
> HEIDI
> You are probably right, but if I get it over now, I'll recover sooner.
> KEVIN
> Yeah, but every time you answer, it reinforces the message it's okay for her to do this to you.
> HEIDI
> I just have to get it over.

Sound familiar? It doesn't just happen with mothers and daughters, but it may occur in any relationship: father-son, siblings, among friends, or in a work setting. The problem with this type of give-and-take relationship is that it goes one way. One person always gives and the other always takes. What makes it worse is the level of disrespect the giver experiences from the demanding an uncaring attitude of the taker. Most of us can tolerate disrespect for a brief moment when we encounter rude people in social situations. However, when the taker is a close connection, say a family member or a friend, the longterm impact of this uneven exchange can take a major toll on the giver.

Take Heidi for example. For her entire life, she had to prove herself to her mother to find approval. It began when she was a little girl with her mother's insistence that she dressed neatly and have a clean, orderly bedroom. Throughout her school years, Heidi's mom expected straight-A's and high performance in piano and dance recitals.

Heidi worked especially hard to achieve her mother's standards, but Mom always seemed to find something Heidi could do better. Privately, Heidi was criticized for minor issues, yet publicly her mother took credit for her success. Her need for her mother's approval, and never quite getting it, drove Heidi to work harder, placing high demands on herself. In her teenage years, Heidi struggled with her self-identity and began experiencing the early onset of anxiety including a brief stint with an eating disorder. Into college, Heidi was driven to succeed, finished top in her class in business management, and after graduation landed a nice-paying job.

As an adult woman, married, with children, Heidi thought perhaps her mother would finally acknowledge her accomplishments and affirm her success. Instead, her mother criticized her marriage, interfered in her parenting, and made demands on her time. Now, a mother herself and focusing on building self-esteem in her young children, Heidi found herself becoming more angry at her mother, although she would never express it.

In her elderly years, Heidi's mom became more demanding and guilted her into doing things for her on a moment's notice. At times, when Heidi would try to stand up for herself, her mother would become excessively emotional, hang up on her, and pout for several days until Heidi apologized. Now in her forties, Heidi feels stuck caring for a person who doesn't seem interested in her feelings at all.

Welcome to the Hotel California.

In situations like Heidi's, the concern for many is knowing where to draw the line without being disrespectful themselves. Sometimes, people can provoke bad behavior in others because everyone has limits. However, is it worth stooping down to the other person's level? It's like getting into a spraying contest with a skunk. In the end, you both stink.

The challenge for individuals like Heidi is to find a way to modify the relationship, to minimize the potential of harm, or in this case, disrespect. The issue here is personal boundaries and self-respect. When a person is being treated poorly, rudely, or in an abusive manner of some sort, they have to decide how much disrespect they want to tolerate. You cannot change a skunk into a rabbit. A skunk is a skunk. You just have to keep enough distance from it so you don't get sprayed.

So often, people try to change others into being something they are not willing to be on their own. Heidi believed if she were perfect, she could win her mother's approval and receive the affirmation she longed for. Often her mother would find something to criticize. The problem wasn't Heidi lacking perfection. The reality was that her mother always put her needs before others; her need to be right, to look good, to have things go her way. In short, her mother was a taker and raised Heidi to be a giver, a perfect compliment to her need for control.

Identifying unhealthy relational patterns is not easy when you are in one. It is much easier to see them in others than ourselves. Often, it takes feedback from those we trust to help us see when we are enmeshed in an unhealthy relationship. Even so, some people have a hard time getting out of toxic relationships. The guilt and sense of duty has a strong gravitational pull that resists change.

This was why it was difficult for Heidi to set limits with her mother. It was ingrained in her thinking from her childhood that her mother came first and failure to meet her expectations would result in a consequence. The punishment as a child or teenager could be a loss of privilege. Yet, on a deeper level, the threat was an unconscious fear of rejection or abandonment. These threats take root in infancy or early childhood and become powerful forces in parent-child attachments. Inevitably, into her adulthood, Heidi still struggles standing up to her mother.

Reciprocity is one of the key elements of respectful relationships. It is the ebb and flow, give and take exchange that happens between two or more people that constitutes a healthy bond. If one makes a kind gesture, the other should reciprocate in like manner. If I listen to your point of view, it would be expected that you would listen to mine. If I do something nice for you, it would be fitting that you reciprocate with a thank you or a kind gesture in return. Reciprocity balances giving and receiving for all parties involved. When reciprocity is absent, the balance of power shifts to the taker, leaving the giver feeling a loss of respect because their needs are not being met. If this uneven pattern develops, resentment is likely to build in the giver and can set a negative tone in the relationship.

Types Of One-Sided Relationships

Set-In-Their-Ways People

These are individuals who see a world of black and white, no shades of gray. They have a hard time seeing things from other people's perspectives. Consequently, they tend to be inflexible, rigid, and controlling in interpersonal relationships. This pattern may emerge from various sources. For example, it may stem from values espoused by one generation that differ from the values of another. People born in the forties and fifties were raised with different notions about male and female roles. Men ruled the house and women ruled the children, creating a three-level hierarchy. Wives deferred to their husbands, acknowledging the power differential that favored men. When the "man of the house" spoke his mind, it became law, no questions asked.

In succeeding generations, with women entering the workforce, the family structure shifted to a two-tier approach with the husband and wife sharing equal power and spousal roles are negotiated. Couples share household duties and decide together most aspects of managing a household and raising kids.

Now, as adult children of the previous generation, they may struggle with parents who think they still know what is best and show no restraint interfering in their lives. Relating to a parent who is set in his or her ways can be difficult, especially when they try to dictate how things should be. Unyielding, they expect you to obey them as adults much like you did when you were children. This usually comes in the form of expectations they impose on your family.

This dynamic can pose problems when adult-children are trying to differentiate their family-of-origin from their family-of-today. Family get-togethers, vacations, and other events can be a source of contention when adult-parents pull rank without regard for the interests of others. We will look at how to handle this type of pattern, but for now let's examine another type of set-in-their-ways people.

Some individuals are set in their ways due to ingrained patterns in their personality or because of the intrusive nature of mental health problems. People who suffer with anxiety or depressive disorders may exhibit patterns of high control and rigidity. On one level, this helps reduce symptoms a little, but on another, it creates huge problems in relationships. Why? Because their need to control their environment includes the people within it. Consequently, they have a hard time yielding to the needs of others and often appear to be insensitive.

Family members lament over the uncaring and self-serving attitude that seems to permeate a relationship with a set-in-their-ways individual. However, for the person with the problem, a disconnect exists between their need for control and their ability to show empathy for the needs of others. It seems too risky to give up control, so they opt for rigidity, leaving the other person wanting support or understanding but not receiving any.

Self-Centered People

Heidi's mom is a classic example of this type of person. Self-centered people exhibit an excessive need for attention. This self-fixation comes at the expense of others getting their needs met. The capacity for this type of individual to care for others is low. Consequently, others are left feeling unimportant, taken advantage of, and resentful. Sadly, our society tends to glamorize this personality style in reality shows, music, and movies. Being selfish, uncaring, and cruel to others is admired as a means for self-promotion and status-ranking in peer settings. This is true not only among adolescents, but in some adult circles.

In interpersonal relationships, self-centered people assume the role of the taker. No surprise here. They can charm their way into your life, yet it ultimately has a self-serving purpose. Before long, you experience the unevenness of the give-and-take dynamic. You are doing all the giving and the self-centered person is doing all the taking. They borrow your things, your money, your clothes, but seem allergic to lending to you. In tough times, they cry on your shoulder, but are unavailable when you need support. In social situations, they absorb attention and may go so far as to ignore you. Yet, on a moment's notice, they will appear on your doorstep needing something from you—time, attention, emotional support. You get the picture.

Self-centered spouses are high maintenance. Laden with narcissism, they view their spouses as an extension of themselves. Consequently, they project their identity needs onto their spouse. This places the marriage in an uneven balance with the demands of one weighing heavily over the needs of the other. Self-centered spouses win most arguments, own most decisions, and enjoy having things go their way. Little concern is shown for their spouse's needs, unless it benefits them in the end.

Partners married to self-centered people often report feeling empty. Years of placating and giving in to the incessant demands of their spouse leaves them feeling resentful and lonely. Many describe a loss of identity, feeling like an empty shell, worthless, and spent. They put up with so much during the course of a marriage, hoping things will be different, but the result is always the same. Disillusionment sets in, followed by despair, then finally divorce. This is the trend I see in marriages with a self-centered spouse.

Suck-You-Dry People

The third type of relationship where respect is not reciprocal are individuals who inflict harm on others. This harm can be physical, psychological, or emotional. I refer to these as Suck-You-Dry (SYD) people. The term may seem extreme, yet in my experience people in this category lack the components that describe a healthy soul. In their core, suck-you-dry people lack a moral compass; they possess no genuine feeling for others. Empathy is absent or contrived for self-serving purposes. These are individuals with little or no conscience to guide their behavior.

Suck-you-dry people have a chameleon-like trait to their personality that attracts them to others. These people are hard to detect because they are the ultimate manipulators, with the ability to perform acts that have others convinced they are genuine. However, this is a ploy on their part to lure unsuspecting victims in. In the early phase of a relationship, they can appear to be kind, caring, and giving, i.e. the traits of a respectful person. Over time, these individuals start showing their true colors.

More than self-centered, their disregard of others can take an aggressive form when necessary. People are viewed as objects of possession and therefore exist to serve the needs of the soul-sucking individual. If the person does not deliver what they expect, a suck-you-dry person can turn on them quickly. When slighted, and this is usually a misperception, they become enraged and retaliate in a harmful fashion to a degree that doesn't fit the crime. Retaliation may take the form of silence, a coldness towards the perceived offender that suggests they committed a huge crime. Other forms of retaliation may be verbal lashing, vandalism, physical harm, or public vilification.

SYDs don't simply suck others dry. They gut them. Others are safe as long as they don't cross them. However, once they do something wrong, cross-hairs appear and they are now an enemy. The unsuspecting person may not know they are a target until they experience a hit, sometimes delayed, coming from the suck-you-dry person. Often blindsided by the attack, the person is left reeling from the hit and feeling unsafe in the relationship.

Suck-you-dry people will use whatever means necessary to do the harm they think the other person deserves. They will lie, invent stories, create a crime scene, whatever it takes to exact revenge. To justify their actions and build support, SYDs will triangulate relationships, often getting mutual friends or family members to support their cause. By weaving a web of deceit, they gain sympathy from others who mistakenly believe the person has been harmed, when in fact they are inflicting the harm via the ruse they created. The true victim is vilified, suffering further harm by being ostracized by others.

Sound too crazy to be true? It happens every day. In my profession, I hear stories like this quite often. Individuals who suffer under a relationship with a SYD often appear traumatized, empty, and powerless. They describe feeling lost, as if they don't know who they are anymore. Understandably so. Individuals in a close relationship with a SYD suffer loss of identity. Other losses may include finances, ties to family members, their health, their career, and their friendships. Sadly, their existence is reduced to an orbit around the massive ego of the suck-you-dry person.

Maintaining Self-Respect In A Disrespectful Relationship

The three types of relationships I described do not offer mutual respect. Sorry to disappoint, but one-sided people are not equipped with this standard. Being in a relationship with an individual who fits one of these categories places you in a difficult position. What's at stake is your self-respect. If you are constantly giving in to the expectations of the taker and not getting anything in return, this will push on your boundary of self-respect. The more you give in to others, the less of you remains.

Let me illustrate in the following diagrams. A healthy relationship is the merging of two independent people into an interdependent relationship. The success of this relationship is determined by two things. First, it is the ability of each individual to maintain a clear expression of their self-identity. Second, success is determined by the respect each person shows to the individuality of the other. Notice how the intersection of the circles depicts boundaries that allow the independence of each individual without one person absorbing the other.

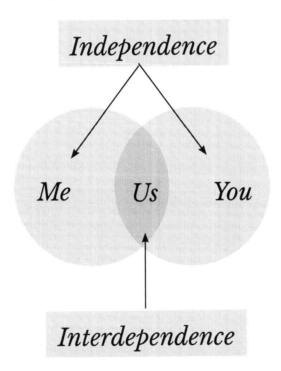

By contrast, in a one-sided relationship, the needs of one person dominate the needs of the other, resulting in absorption. In psychology, this is what is referred to as a symbiotic relationship. The danger of this type of relational pattern is the loss of identity that happens to one individual in favor of the demanding identity needs of the other. In this type of relationship, mutual respect is unattainable.

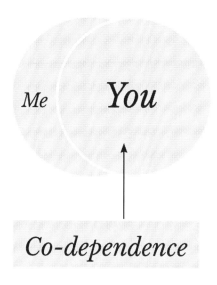

Maintaining self-respect in a relationship with someone who does not show you respect is not easy. You will likely be pitted in struggles for control over issues you shouldn't have to fight over. This dance of disrespect can wear on you over time. You may be tempted to give in to avoid conflict, to keep the peace. Know this: Constantly giving in means giving up your self-respect.

The important thing to remember is how valuable self-respect is to your quality of life. If you give up your right to choose, your right to use your voice, your right to your interests, wants, and needs, then you no longer exist for yourself. You forfeit your right to be you. Instead, you choose to live a life others expect you to live.

One of my favorite movies is *October Sky*. It is based on a true story about the Rocket Boys, four teenagers who lived in a coal-mining town in Coalwood, West Virginia. These high schoolers, led by Homer Hickman, Jr., won the 1960 National Science Fair with their presentation on propulsion, based on their experiments with homemade rockets. Homer, like most boys growing up in a coal mining town, was expected to work in the mines, just like his father Homer, Sr..

Prior to the science fair, Homer's father, a "set-in-his ways" personality, orders his son to give up his silly notions about playing with rockets and to go back and work in the coal mine.

Homer looks at his father and says, "Dad, the coal mine is your life. I'm going into space."

With that, Homer sets his gaze to the sky and forges ahead with his goal, which ultimately leads him to work at NASA. His father eventually came to understand his son and respect his choice. This would not have happened had Homer not used his voice to stand up to his father about his chosen path.

I cannot overstate how important it is in bringing respect back into your life that you begin with your self-respect. Knowing who you are and being clear with yourself and others is important going forward. As you begin to advocate for your passions, needs, and purposes while balancing this with respect for others, you will live a meaningful life.

Along the way, you will have to face off against people whose expectations for you conflict with your expectations for yourself. Their opposition may pressure you to conform just to keep peace or not forfeit the relationship. You may feel disrespected by their disregard for what is important to you. How will you handle this? What do you do in relationships with people who do not reciprocate respect? Here are some things to consider when you are in a relationship that doesn't offer the respect you give.

Grieve The Relationship You Envisioned

Many of us go into adult relationships with certain expectations of how we want our lives to be. For those seeking marriage and a family, there is the hope of a solid partnership, healthy and happy children, and perhaps a slice of the American dream. This sounds reasonable, but for many, the dream turns into a nightmare.

Perhaps you can relate to one of the following scenarios. The spouse who's always known the right things to say and do to make you feel special suddenly does all the wrong things, leaving you feeling like you don't matter. The parent you've tried so hard to please for forty years is still unsatisfied, leaving you wondering if you will ever hear the words, I love you and I am proud of you. The children you sacrificed so much for routinely miss your birthday, blame you for their problems, and call you only when they need something.

The breakdown of the family in America is not a recent trend. The cumulative effect of the disintegration of the family institution in our country over the past fifty years has been alarming. More than half of all marriages end in divorce. The divorce rate in second marriages is higher. Infidelity, addiction, alcoholism, abuse, and other maladaptive behaviors erode marriages daily. Adult children of divorce are leery of marriage. Mental health problems abound in homes due to high stress levels in familial relationships. Some individuals hold family members hostage with their chaotic behavior. For families that crave happiness, the obstacles abound.

In the case of Heidi, she eventually had to come to terms with her relationship with her mom. The relationship she hoped to have is not likely to happen unless her mother goes through a radical change on the inside. Her mother lacks the sensitivity and compassion necessary to meet the relational needs of her daughter. Heidi has to let this vision go and grieve the relationship she hoped to have with her mother. As long as she keeps it alive, she sets herself up for more hurt. Once she lets it go, she can accept the reality that her mom cannot consistently give her the love she needs.

For those who are in a relationship with a person I described earlier as stuck in their ways, self-centered, or suck-you-dry, you are not going to experience the reciprocity of respect on a normal basis. You might receive rare moments of it, but do not assume this will become a norm. To protect your heart from hope deferred, you will have to accept the fact that you will not get a steady diet of affirmation. Grieve the dream of what you have hoped for and accept what you have. You cannot make people love you, nor can you make them show they care. It has to come from within them. If you haven't been successful over all the years you've tried, you are better off letting go of the dream and accepting reality. For whatever reason—a bad childhood, overindulgent parents—the person is unable to give you what you want. You cannot make it happen. Let it go.

Grieving the dream of a relationship you wished for is not a simple decision, it's a process. Forgiveness is a key element in the process. Recently, I wrote an article entitled, *"Forgiving from a Distance"*. I wrote this in response to a question I am often asked: "How do I resolve feelings of anger and hurt from a person who wronged me and is unwilling to repair the offense?"

Sometimes we experience deep hurts in interpersonal relationships. What often exacerbates the problem is a refusal on the part of the offender to acknowledge, accept responsibility, and attempt to repair the wound. This leaves the wounded person in the position of having to bring closure to the matter alone.

Unacknowledged, non-repaired offenses often perpetuate the pain suffered by individuals like Heidi, who are on the receiving end. Untreated emotional wounds often hamper the injured, leaving them with feelings of anger and bitterness. Furthermore, they may have difficulty trusting or letting others get close to them.

Forgiving people from a distance is not for the benefit of the offender; it is for the benefit of the injured. The residual effects of unresolved offenses only hurt you. Think about the individuals who hurt you without repairing the offense. Notice how they go on with their lives as if nothing is wrong?

Holding on to unresolved offenses perpetuates the harm caused by the person who hurt you. Being angry and bitter gives them indirect power over your life. Think about it. When you dwell on the offense, wishing for revenge, or waiting for an apology, you give them control over your thoughts and feelings from a distance. Dwelling can lead to health problems, low self esteem, and depression. Forgiving from a distance is for you, not the offender.

Forgiving from a distance is a threefold process of letting out, letting go, and letting in. Letting out involves a deliberate exercise of releasing feelings, pent up emotions, and thoughts you have about the person and what they have done to you. This can be done several ways. One of the best ways is to simply write, type, or journal your thoughts and feelings. In one session you can release the root cause of your anger. Scribe until you have exhausted yourself of the feeling of anger. Underneath the anger, you will likely experience other emotions such as fear, sadness, loneliness, and hurt. As you write, allow these feelings an outlet as well.

After you let out your anger, you can begin the second part of the process, letting go of the emotion. You can do this as a prayer, giving it to God, or you can choose some other symbolic method of releasing the anger. Be creative in your exercise of letting go, as long as it is not hurtful to yourself or others.

Finally, let in something good in place of the bad you released. It may be as simple as doing a fun activity, going out for dinner with friends, having a massage, or taking a nature walk. Letting in may also include journaling about the lessons you have learned from your experiences, how it made you stronger.

Recently, I talked with a young man who had a difficult childhood. As he was going through this process of grieving his childhood and forgiving from a distance, he talked about a few of the benefits he gained from those early years. He shared how those experiences helped him develop a sense of maturity and self-responsibility which have served him well in his transition into adulthood. Extracting some good from the past fills the void left by the anger and the hurt.

Adjust Your Expectations For The Relationship

Once you grieve the relationship you have wanted, you are free from the anxiety of trying to make it happen. Now you are ready to adjust your expectations. This involves some rethinking and lowering the bar of expectations for the individual you were looking to for love. No longer will you expect a thoughtful gesture, compliment, or expression of concern. When it doesn't happen, you may experience slight disappointment, but not the deep hurt you are accustomed to feeling.

Over time, Heidi learned to lower her expectations of what she was going to get from her mom. She stopped looking for her mother's approval. This simple act was freeing for Heidi. It released her from feeling anxiety and guilt. She could also tolerate her mother's self-centeredness without becoming upset.

Lowering the bar of expectations is beneficial because you are no longer looking for something you are not going to get. Consequently, you are not distraught when the person's actions fit the familiar pattern. You might be disappointed, but this emotion is easier to tolerate. This adjustment sets you up for the next step—modifying your boundaries.

Modify Your Boundaries Accordingly

As I discussed in previous chapters, personal boundaries are important in establishing respectful relationships. They are even more critical when you are in a relationship with a disrespectful person. Weak boundaries allow disrespectful people to walk into your life and take advantage of you. To regain control and your self-respect, you will have to modify the boundaries you have with people in unhealthy relationships.

Boundaries should not be modified out of retaliation for being hurt. Rather, they are set as a healthy measure to regain control of your life and hopefully help the relationship function more appropriately. In establishing boundaries with others, you are clarifying what you can and cannot do. Boundaries also communicate to others how you expect to be treated.

Modifying Boundaries with Self-Centered People

To break the pattern of her mother's self-centeredness, Heidi learned how to say No to her. Instead of dropping everything to attend to her mother's demands, Heidi took a moment to think the decision through without worrying about her mother's response. Because she had previously done the work of grieving the relationship she had dreamed of and adjusting her expectations, modifying her boundaries with her mother was done with minimal angst.

Notice Heidi did not cut her mother off completely. When she was available, Heidi helped her mom, and she continued to have a relationship with her. When her mother pouted or became angry at Heidi for not doing what she expected, Heidi did not come undone. She understood that she was not responsible for her mother's feelings. This freed her from the guilt and resentment she had previously when she was controlled by her mother's emotional reactions.

Over time, Heidi's mother learned to respect the boundaries. Sometimes, she even caught herself in the middle of a ploy to get her way and stopped herself from trying to manipulate Heidi. There were moments in the relationship when things were intense, but her mom seemed to rebound. On her part, Heidi tried to be fair and not overuse the No. In the end, the relationship improved and her mother would even show some gratitude on occasion. Heidi enjoyed these moments, knowing they were rare, but she could see her mom was trying. Years later, when her mother passed away, Heidi was able to grieve with less resentment about the past and more fond memories about the final years of their life together.

Modifying Boundaries with Set-In-Their-Ways People

If you are in a relationship with a person who is set in their ways, modifying boundaries with them is also challenging work. Their rigidity can hurt you. To maintain control over your life, a firm No is in order. Clarifying boundaries in a polite, yet firm manner with adult-parents informs them that you are in charge of your life, not them. Remember, most people get over their hurt feelings after a while. Letting them stew a little is not such a bad thing, especially if in the end, you maintain control of your life and your family.

What is particularly challenging is modifying boundaries with set-in-their-ways spouses. You may see adult parents on occasion, but a spouse who is set in their ways lives with you every day! Living with a rigid spouse can be a daily ordeal of walking on eggshells. The spouses' need for order and control makes them demanding, inflexible, and harsh toward others who do not align with their way of thinking. Minor issues easily become major battles due to their low frustration tolerance.

Setting boundaries with a rigid spouse does require adaptive skill that accomplishes two things: you assuage their intense emotion while you also hold firm to your position on a matter. Keep in mind that in most cases, people who possess rigid traits have an underlying current of anxiety that governs their life. You may experience their secondary emotion, say anger, while their primary emotion of anxiety throbs below the surface.

Anxiety-based disorders such as obsessive-compulsive disorder are characterized by a form of rigidity that orders an individual's world, thereby mitigating threats and lowering anxiety. A set-in-their-ways spouse expresses rigidity not to be a jerk, but to keep their anxiety from wreaking havoc in their minds. Therefore, in establishing boundaries with your spouse, it is important that you use stress-reducing language to lower his or her anxiety while you advocate for your position. Let me illustrate.

Tom and Jill were having a cup of coffee when their eleven year-old daughter Caitlyn came running into the kitchen and announced she was invited by their neighbors Alex and Karen Wilson, to go to the water park with their family for the day. Tom's immediate response was a sharp No to the invitation.

When Caitlyn asked for a reason, her father said, "You are not going to a place where something bad could happen to you. Don't bother asking again, the answer is no!"

Caitlyn left the room in tears and slammed her bedroom door.

Jill looked over at Tom and with a calm demeanor said, "I can see you're worried something bad might happen to Caitlyn."

"Of course, Jill!" Tom said. "She could get injured on one of the slides or drown. Besides, you know how easy it would be for someone to abduct her? I know Alex and Karen will be watching over the kids, but come on. They can't see everything that's going on."

Jill reached over and placed her hand on top of Tom's and said, "Honey, I can see that you don't want to place your daughter in harm's way. It would kill you if you gave her permission to go and something bad happened to her. On the other hand, by denying Caitlyn opportunities for safe fun you are hurting her a different way. I don't agree with your decision and I think we need to revisit it and come up with a plan that allows her to go. If it will ease your mind, maybe you or I can go along."

Tom thought for a moment and said, "Maybe I was overreacting a bit. Let's talk with the Wilsons about their plans for the day at the water park and ask them to be sure to keep an eye on Caitlyn."

With a kiss on the cheek, Jill says, "Good idea."

Notice how Jill adopts a stress-reducing position with Tom? She doesn't react to his anger and uptightness. Rather, she focuses on the primary emotion of worry that lies beneath the surface of his expressed anger. By validating Tom's fear, it helps to lower the intensity of his anxiety, which will give her more leverage to appeal to his sense of reason. Furthermore, Jill expresses her disagreement with Tom and points out how his actions are hurting his daughter. Standing firm on her opposition to his choice and inviting Tom to dialog with her more about the matter influenced him to rethink his position and acknowledge he was overreacting, a common behavior among rigid people.

Modifying Boundaries with Suck-You-Dry People

Sometimes people have to take drastic measures in boundary modification, especially if it concerns individuals whose behavior is harmful to the well-being of others. Suck-you-dry (SYD) people do not know how to live in healthy relationships. Their toxic traits are lethal in a family. Individuals living in a family environment with a poisonous person often live in great fear. They do not want to do anything that will ignite the ire of the person. Consequently, they feel stuck in a situation they fear they cannot escape. To cope, they do whatever they can to appease the suck-you-dry person.

Boundaries are not permissible in a relationship with a SYD person, at least on their terms. They may give a little wiggle room, but not enough to honor personal freedom. When you are out, they want to know where, with whom, and how long. They may incessantly text or call you while away for no apparent reason other than to monitor your whereabouts and keep your attention on them. Suck-you-dry people will make you feel guilty for leaving them alone or outside without inviting them. The subtle message in their demeanor suggests you are not allowed to have a good time and should feel guilty for leaving them, even for a short time.

Escaping from a SYD person may be like leaving the Mafia. Be prepared to face a punishment. They will use all forms of manipulation and threats to keep you from leaving. Charm, gifts, or some form of indulgence is an initial ploy. If this doesn't work, they may promise not to be so controlling if you would be more caring, as a means to guilt you into staying. Finally, if these don't work, a SYD person may use psychological or physical threats of punishment to control you.

If you live in a relationship with someone who uses extreme forms of manipulation with the threat of psychological, emotional, or physical harm, it is important that you reach out for help. Talk with someone outside the family circle. Seek individual counseling to help you assess your situation, get support, and find an appropriate means to confront the problem. You may feel scared or that you are betraying the SYD person. These are normal feelings under the circumstances. However, it is important that you reach out for help.

Fill The Void With Healthy Relationships

I have found when individuals establish boundaries with others, one of two things will likely happen. One is that others will adjust to the boundaries you set in order to preserve the relationship (except in the case of a SYD person). This of course is what most people hope will happen. As a result, the relationships become stronger or at least more respectful.

The second outcome is not as favorable. Unfortunately, some individuals will not respect your boundaries. Instead, they will test them to determine if you are serious or just complaining. If they can get you to give up your boundaries, then they will stay in the relationship. On the other hand, if your boundaries are firm, some individuals will exit the relationship. Albeit sad, this is not necessarily a bad thing. It simply says that the person did not value the relationship enough to accommodate your reasonable request. When this happens, a void opens up.

If you are ridding yourself of unhealthy relationships, then you may want to consider filling the void with healthy ones. There are plenty of good people in the world who can be a dependable friend, a surrogate parent, or a caring sibling. They may not share your genetic code, but if they share your core values and know how to reciprocate respect, you can form a healthy bond. The important thing is you take your time, do your homework, and give the relationship time to prove it is what you are looking for.

Support groups, small groups in church settings, or social clubs can be settings where you can develop healthy relationships. Some find themselves adopted into the larger family of a close friend. Holidays, birthdays, and anniversaries are celebrated as if the individual was born into the family. As you begin working on bringing self-respect back into your life, this will open the door to new experiences and opportunities to meet people.

Let's say for example you decide that in improving self-care, you want to exercise by bicycling. You discover that a bicycle club is starting in your local community health center. Here is an opportunity to do something that addresses your self-care needs and social interest. Developing friendships with others who are concerned about health aligns with your values and provides opportunity for relationship.

I could give several other examples, but I think you understand my point. Fill the void left by individuals who don't show you respect by developing new relationships with people who will. Look around: surrogate relationships abound among those who have suffered loss of love, friendship, or family. You don't have to live in social isolation, nor should you concede to the expectations of people who don't reciprocate. Step out of your comfort zone and try something new.

Taking Action

One-sided relationships are the hardest to navigate, especially when you want to exit.[9] Sheryl Crow addresses this insanity in her 1998 hit single "Anything But Down". Takers will do almost anything to keep you in the relationship, playing on your finest asset--being a nice person. However, I have seen nice people gradually become resentful when they have been taken advantage of for too long. Multiple appeals to address the problem are ignored. The dance remains the same. Over time, one-sided relationships become stale. Giving without getting something back gets old. Tired of a one-sided dance, givers become resentful. Gradually, emotional distancing establishes geographical space. Separateness defines the relationship. The giver gives less. Their will to work on the relation-

---

9   Album: The Globe Sessions, 1998

ship weakens. Resentment takes over and all the reasons for staying no longer make sense. What's left is finding the courage to take action.

If you are in a one-sided relationship that is causing emotional, psychological, or physical harm, I urge you to do something to begin getting your self-respect back. Perhaps you feel stuck or maybe trapped in the relationship. I suggest you reach out for help. Find someone to talk to who can give you support and solid advice. It may also be beneficial to seek professional help to unpack this problem, get support, and find solutions that work for you. Doing nothing will not solve the problem. It will perpetuate it. You stand much to lose by inaction. Taking action will give you control back in your life.

For most people, change comes with some level of trepidation. Many questions emerge. "Am I making the right decision?" "Will it work out in the end?" "Am I rushing?" "Will it get better over time?" When we are afraid it is easy to talk ourselves out of things we know we need to do. Emotional reasoning is probably not a good approach here. You would be better served to allow your thinking part of the brain to lead the way.

Below are a seven questions you might want to ask yourself. The list is not exhaustive. You may come up with more questions to add. I recommend you write your answers down in order to gain clarity on the matter. Your answers will likely inform you on where you stand and what your next steps may be going forward.

"What is wrong with this relationship?"
"How is it affecting my life?"
"What has been done to try to correct the problem?"
"Has it worked?"
"Have I exhausted all my options/solutions to correct the problem?"
"What can I expect will happen if I continue this way?"
"How will my life be different if I exit out of the relationship?

Now that you have finished this exercise, I want you to think about how you might take action. For givers in one-sided relationships, decisions are generally based on the expectation of the takers in their life. It is time now for you to think about yourself. In order to do this you must shift your brain from an external focus (taker) to an internal focus (self). No, this is not a selfish exercise! It is an exercise in self-care. I leave you with ten statements to reflect on. Read them slowly. Internalize them as truth statements. May they give you both the insight and courage to act.

"I matter."

"My needs are important."

"I have a right to my thoughts."

"I have a right to my feelings."

"I have a right to speak and be heard."

"I have a right to decide for myself."

"I choose to respect myself."

"I expect others to respect me."

"I will not allow myself to be in a relationship with someone who does not show me respect."

"I have the courage to advocate for what I want in life."

Chapter Ten

What You Can Expect When Respect Happens

Kevin, Heidi, and Stacey find seats in the high school auditorium that is steadily filling up with other families eager to get a good seat before the ceremony begins. As Kevin checks the battery power on his video camera, he leans to Heidi and whispers, "Did you ever think this day would come?"

"I had my doubts" Heidi says. "I think Brandon might have surprised himself!"

The Hughes were about to watch their son graduate from high school.

Brandon struggled all four years of high school. His sophomore and junior years were the hardest. Coincidentally, these were the worst years in the Hughes household. Kevin and Heidi's marriage was hanging by a thread, Brandon and Stacey were constantly at each other's throats, and the home was in a perpetual state of chaos. Brandon pulled away from his family, everyone for that matter, except for a few friends, all of whom his parents did not like or trust.

During those two years, Brandon advanced to the next grade level by a razor-thin margin. By all indications, it seemed highly likely that Brandon would drop out of school. He hated it, protesting regularly with his parents and teachers that it was a waste of time. In class, he was bored, disinterested, and rarely participated except to disrupt the classroom with a joke or insult to a teacher he didn't like. Often, Brandon would come to school stoned on weed he had smoked on the way with his friends. Every year he was absent beyond the quota, except for his senior year when he started turning things around.

Brandon's attitude toward school changed when things started to change at home. It didn't happen right away, but as his family started showing respect to each other, the tension in the home decreased and everyone started liking each other again. The battle to get him up for school in the morning ended and Brandon started to take responsibility for getting himself to school. There were a few setbacks, but the way he and his parents handled them made it easier to get back on track. Before long, Brandon started paying attention, engaged in classroom discussion, and did his homework. His GPA reached a respectable 2.5, not to mention an A in computer science and art. Brandon shocked his parents when he told them he wanted to go to a community college, "To see if I like it," and possibly transfer to a school with a program in computer animation.

As you can see, the Hughes have come a long way since we observed the family dynamics in the first chapter. As you may recall, the school issue was a war between Brandon and his parents. Kevin avoided it, having checked out of his parental duties. Heidi was locked into a battle of wills with Brandon, emotionally scarred by the psychological warfare she encountered every day. When the Hughes family decided to bring respect back into the family, the dynamics changed and family members started caring for each other. Individuals took responsibility for their actions and, in doing so, were able to work through their problems and became goal-directed.

Bringing respect back in your personal life and interpersonal relationships will yield positive results. Respect generates a sense of well-being, and produces goodness, compassion, and kindness, among other qualities of greatness. If you act in this manner toward yourself and others, the outcome will be good. You will have a heightened sense of self-worth and self-confidence. When you show respect toward others, they will accept you and allow you into their circle of trust. In this final chapter, I would like to highlight several benefits you can expect to receive when you bring respect back into your life.

Refined Sense Of Self

To refine something involves removing the impurities or unwanted properties and enhancing the natural elements that accentuate its inherent worth. Every human is born with a core that is inherently good. Life has the ability to corrupt this goodness through the experience of living in community with others. We are imperfect people who live in an imperfect world. Over the course of time, these imperfections skew our view of ourselves and others. Along the way, many of us lose our self-respect.

In the chapter on bringing self-respect back, I discussed the importance of being good to yourself by addressing your inner core in a manner of self-acceptance, self-care, and self-responsibility. When individuals get serious about taking care of themselves, self-respect emerges as the defining value. Self-respect gives energy and motivation to the effort of doing good, living healthy, and establishing personal boundaries. Bad habits give way to healthy choices, from dieting to dating.

For me, regaining my self-respect occurred in a period of my life that was very difficult. I was going through major change after a painful loss. It seemed like my whole world was changing and, in some respects, I felt out of control. I was experiencing intense feelings of anger, betrayal, confusion, loneliness, and fear. No doubt, I felt vulnerable to these emotions, but I could not check out of life. I still had responsibilities to take care of and critical decisions to make in this period of transition.

This was not a time for me to wallow in self-pity or act irresponsibly by doing my own thing and making excuses—although I have to admit it was tempting. Rather, it became a time for healing, self-reflection, and reconnecting with myself. I chose to work on me while surrounding myself with a small circle of trusted family and friends I could count on for support and to keep me accountable. Looking back, it was a wise move on my part to remain close to trusted family members and friends. They knew me well and could help me get a better read on my situation that was in part distorted by the painful emotions I was experiencing at the time.

During this phase, I worked hard on regaining my self-respect. Major areas of my life were unsettled, with family and career at the top of the list. Emotionally, I was really beat up at that time. My self-esteem was at an all-time low and I wasn't helping the matter with all the negativity I was heaping upon myself. Since I had a tendency to blame myself for everything that goes wrong, self-respect was hard to find. Externally, I could perform my duties, but internally, I was a mess.

As I took time to reflect, I learned about patterns in my life that were not healthy. Consequently, I began to work on changing them and developing new ways to interact with others. One of the areas needing attention were my personal boundaries. Being a people-pleaser, I was trying to gain approval by doing what I thought others expected from me. By establishing limits for myself and others, I started to gain more control over my life and I felt more peace.

I also took inventory on what attributes, interests, and passions really defined my sense of self. Having clarity on who I was helped point me in the direction I wanted to go in life. This refined sense of self also gave me a new aim in life, which eventually led to my work in mental health.

If you were to ask me where to start in bringing respect back into your life, I would say begin with your self-respect. So often, we tolerate disrespect because we do not have enough respect for ourselves to stand up to others. By following the steps I suggest in chapter three, you will be in the process of gaining a refined sense of self.

Keener Sense Of Purpose & Direction

Being clear on who you are as a person gives you a keener sense of what you want out of life. People who lack self-respect are more likely to have no sense of purpose in life. Nor do they seem to know where they want to go. As a result, they tend to rely on others for direction or may be more inclined to take the path of least resistance. Lacking personal boundaries, they may defer their right to chart their course to someone in their life who likes to call the shots. Consequently, they end up living in someone else's dream, which can turn out to be a nightmare. The forfeiture of one's sense of purpose may leave them feeling empty—aimless wanderers.

Bringing self-respect back not only refines your self-identity; it also gives you clarity on what you want to become. This includes both the smaller and the larger purposes of your life. On the smaller purposes, you may find yourself doing things on your bucket list that you haven't taken the time to pursue. This includes new hobbies, activities, or adventures you always wanted to experience.

When I was bringing self-respect back in my life, one of the items on my list was traveling to Europe. I purchased a book by Rick Steves, *Europe Through the Back Door*, and began reading and dreaming about some of the places I wanted to visit. A friend of mine, who is an artist and potter, made me a euro bank, a container with a map of Europe on the top, to start saving for my trip. During this time, I decided to go back to school to get an advanced degree in counseling. To my surprise, upon my graduation, a friend I had helped through a very difficult time, gifted me and my wife with a three-week trip to Europe.

Notice the small and big ticket items that emerged when I started bringing respect back in my life. The small ticket item was a trip to Europe. The large ticket item was a return to academia as a means to launch a new career. Over time, items were checked off and new items appeared. For example, I discovered in grad school a talent—although green—for writing. I was encouraged by my professors to consider publishing. Within a few years, I was able to publish as a contributing author in clinical literature. This current project, my first book to the general public, is the latest expression of my life's purpose to help people.

When you get a grip on yourself, the future is easier to navigate. Decisions will come more easily from within you than from what others expect you to do. The achievement of personal goals leads toward a meaningful life and enriching relationships. Most importantly, you will have a sense of inner peace because you are living your life.

A Healthier Lifestyle — Less Stress And More Energy

Getting your self-respect back may have a ripple effect—a pleasant one, I might add. It permeates all areas of your life. One of the things you may notice is a greater sense of control over how you live your daily life. What you may experience is a shift in your locus of control from external to internal. Individuals with an external locus of control make the majority of their decisions to satisfy the expectations of others. On the other hand, people with an internal locus of control decide from within, choosing what they think is best for themselves.

In a healthy lifestyle, decisions come from an internal locus of control, a sense of knowing what you want and not simply doing things to gain approval or avoid disapproval from others. Evidence of the shift from an external to internal control will manifest in the use of boundary-marking decisions. Boundaries are simple rules based on personal values. Establishing boundaries for yourself and others reduces stress and promotes health. Let me explain.

Let's say that in bringing self-respect back, you identify specific values you want to integrate into your life. Among these are a healthy body and healthy relationships. Taking a personal inventory, you note that you have poor eating habits that has resulted in being overweight and fighting high cholesterol. Furthermore, you discover your high stress level comes from too many commitments and not enough time in the day to get everything done. You acknowledge that you have a hard time saying no to requests from others. In your relationships, you are working hard to please others to a point where people take advantage of you and your needs go unmet.

Boundaries with yourself and others will correct these problems. By shifting to an internal locus of control, choosing based on your values and not the approval of others, you will start placing limits on yourself and with people. You may choose to modify your diet to achieve the goal of weight-loss and lowering your cholesterol. In addition, you may add some form of exercise to achieve your healthy lifestyle goal. When given the choice of Ben & Jerry's ice-cream, you may choose the yogurt version of Cherry Garcia over the standard ice-cream selection. By the way, this is an example of one of my personal boundaries. In placing limits with others, you will find yourself declining requests more often when it conflicts with your schedule or does not align with your values. Initially, saying no to people may be awkward and elicit feelings of guilt, but if you hold to your boundary, you will maintain an internal locus of control and experience less stress.

Boundaries are indicators of self-respect. When we place limits on ourselves and with others, the ability to maintain control reduces stress and provides more energy to enjoy life and pursue things of interest. I like to say that boundaries help me be the me I want to be. There is a sense of inner strength that comes from choosing from within and experiencing the benefits in daily life. Interpersonal relationships are less stressful and more meaningful because boundaries keep respect in check. When you bring self-respect back into your life, it also empowers you to be respectful of others without losing yourself. You seek the balance of personal welfare with the welfare of others.

This leads to another benefit of bringing respect back into your life.

Greater Understanding Of Others

One of the biggest barriers in human relations is the lack of understanding between people. The art of listening is more likely to be exercised when getting acquainted with others and less so with people we know. Power plays a role in this. We are less inclined to really listen to someone we are in a relationship with if our sense of power is threatened in an argument or dispute. Instead, we tend to focus on getting our point across and may become defensive or think about our counterpoint while the other person is talking. Over time, patterns of reactive dialog that emphasize speaking over listening reinforce unhealthy communication and leave people frustrated in their relationships.

To break these negative patterns, listening and validating are key. When you take the time to listen to your spouse, child, or sibling and convey to them an understanding of what they are saying without judgment, you have started a respectful dialog. Validation conveys understanding; it is not synonymous with agreement. You can validate a person's point of view without having to agree with it.

As an illustration, consider a spousal discussion where the wife complains that her husband doesn't support her career. He listens to her complaint and responds, "What I hear you saying is you don't think I support your career because I never ask you questions about it."

Allowing his wife a right to her thoughts and feelings conveys respect and gives him a greater understanding of them. Understanding is fundamental to respectful relationships. In this illustration, the husband may very well support his wife's career, but is learning that she wants him to show more interest by engaging her in conversation about it.

Another benefit in understanding others is that you know how to offer a more effective response. When understanding is absent, individuals act on assumptions. A response based on an assumption of what one thinks the other means is more often inaccurate, causing confusion or frustration. Misassumption is the culprit in many arguments between people. However, when individuals take the time to listen well, ask questions, and convey an understanding of what the other person is saying, the response will more likely be helpful in the moment. Let me illustrate how understanding keeps misassumptions from occurring and increases the ability to give an appropriate response.

Heidi comes home from work, surveys the messy kitchen, tosses her keys on the granite counter, and heads upstairs to the master bedroom. Kevin's suitcase is neatly packed, ready for the early flight tomorrow, a couples-only vacation. She heads to the family room where he is melted into his recliner watching the evening news. Heidi heads back to the kitchen to tackle the mess, making noise as she bangs pots and pans in frustration. Hearing the ruckus, Kevin moves toward the kitchen to see what is going on.

He notices a familiar, not too friendly look on Heidi's face and instantly thinks, *Oh crap, she's angry at me because the kitchen is a mess!* His initial thought is to do an about-face and avoid her until the storm settles down. Remembering that avoiding conflict is something he agreed to work on, Kevin decides to approach Heidi and asks, "Hi honey, you doing okay?"

"What does it look like, Kevin? I come home from work the night before we leave for our trip and I'm stuck cleaning the kitchen. I should be packing."

At this point, Kevin feels his defenses kicking in and he is ready to fire back. Instead, he pauses, looks at Heidi, and says, "It sounds like you've had a tough day. Care to tell me about it?"

"It's been horrible, Kevin" Heidi says with tears welling up in her eyes. "My boss dumped a ton of work on me today, and he's been in a nasty mood. I think he does this deliberately every time I am about to go on vacation. Then I come home and find the kitchen a mess. You're packed, I'm not, and you're relaxing in front of the TV."

Fighting a reaction, Kevin says, "I get the sense you feel dumped on today. I'll tell you what. Why don't you go upstairs and take care of packing and then relax in the Jacuzzi for a while? I'll order some Chinese food after I call Stacy and remind her to get her butt home and clean the kitchen. After all, this is her assigned day, not yours, mine, or Brandon's. You want egg rolls with your kung pao?"

Hearing his thoughtful response, Heidi hugs Kevin and he caresses her back while she sheds a few more tears. "It was a rough day, Kevin. Sorry for taking it out on you with my mood. I'm looking forward to some down time with you on this trip."

"Me too."

Notice how Kevin initially assumed he was the cause of Heidi's mood. He was prepared for flight, a strategy he'd employed in the past. When he approached her and caught initial heat, his defenses kicked in and he was ready to snap back at her. Instead, he slowed himself down, kept his mood in check and asked her to tell him what was wrong. He took a position of curiosity and listened for a response. Next, Kevin conveyed an understanding of what Heidi said by summarizing her point in a simple statement, "I get the sense you feel dumped on today." Then he offered a solution that countered her negative feelings and would enhance her mood. Feeling understood and cared for, Heidi was able to *let out* and *let go* of her negative feelings and *let in* some self-care activity to relax and improve her mood. Summarizing, Kevin disarmed a conflict within minutes, saving valuable time and energy for connecting, a wonderful prelude to a romantic getaway!

Validating is challenging when the person you are in conflict with reports things inaccurately or amplifies the problem beyond what transpired. It is especially difficult when the person portrays you or your actions in a manner that is incongruent with how you see yourself. The predictable response is to defend yourself and dispute the person's accusations. However, this reaction not only invalidates the person's thoughts and feelings, but it also amps up the conflict, because now you are both upset.

A more respectful response would be to convey an understanding of what the person must feel in the relationship based on their perspective. A follow-up comment would then be a statement of clarification of your intentions in the matter, how you view your conduct, and your true sentiments toward the person. Let me illustrate how this might work in the Hughes family.

STACY

I hate you Dad! I hate you! You are so controlling. You treat me like a two year-old! All my friends get to stay out past curfew. Their parents don't mind. You don't trust me! You think I'm going to get into trouble. I'm not Brandon, you know! All of a sudden you start acting like a parent. Where were you before? This is a big facade. You're doing this parent stuff so mom doesn't divorce you and you won't have to pay child support. I don't buy it. You haven't changed. I don't want you to be my dad.

KEVIN

I can see you're angry at me, in fact you may not even like me. You think I'm doing this to protect myself from divorce. It must make you feel unimportant and unloved. I get it. I probably deserve some of your anger for not being a good father to you for so long. I'm sorry you feel this way. What I do want you to know is that I am here because I love my family. I understand you may not like my rule about curfew but I am doing this not because I don't trust you, but because I care about you and want to protect you. The curfew won't always be in place, but it is for now. You can be mad at me. I understand. You're my daughter and I choose to be your dad because I love you, pure and simple.

When people amplify a problem, the tendency to dispute or correct their view will only make the situation worse. Kevin did not correct his daughter. He allowed Stacy to express her view and sentiment toward him without correction. Furthermore, he did not become reactive or show anger toward her. Instead, he extracted a kernel of truth in her statement about his absenteeism as a dad and owned it. Afterwards, he clarified for Stacy his true intentions and sentiments toward her. This defused the argument and left her with an alternative view of him to consider. Understanding how she feels toward him will enable Kevin to further modify his actions toward her, which will likely facilitate a closer relationship over time.

Taking a non-reactive approach when conflict erupts at you is not an easy task. Our natural instinct is to defend-attack. The key to a non-defensive, stress-reducing response begins with self-control. You have to quickly gain composure of yourself by focusing in, not out on the other person. In essence, you have to slow things down.

There is a scene in the movie *The Matrix*, where the main character, Neo, is being shot at by a man wielding a gun. To protect himself from imminent danger, Neo observes the scene in slow motion, whereby he is able to dodge bullets using carefully choreographed movements. Wouldn't it be nice to possess that skill? Simply put, it is important to slow things down, especially yourself when you are in conflict setting. Doing so will give you a more accurate read on what is coming your way—anger, blame, etc… and provide a more useful, disarming response in the situation.

Here are a few simple steps to slow things down in order to give a respectful response to defuse a conflict. First, take a deep breath, slowly breathing in from your diaphragm for five seconds, hold for two, and release for another five seconds. If possible, do this a few more times. This process allows you to get control of your brain, which is in a fight-flight mode. Second, while you are breathing, become aware of your emotion and its intensity. You might say to yourself, *Right now I am really angry and want to give this person a piece of my mind.* Third, calmly and silently, talk yourself down from the intensity of your anger. *I am angry, but will wait, listen and try to understand what the other person has to say.* Fourth, go back to listening to the person, track their emotions and validate their feelings. *I understand you are angry at me because I would not let you stay out past curfew.* Lastly, once you have lowered the intensity of the conflict by slowing things down and validating the other person, you can offer a respectful response to the conflict.

Improved Communication And Conflict Resolution Skills

Respect creates a safe space for individuals to communicate. When an atmosphere allows free expression of one's thoughts or feelings without criticism or attack, communication flows rhythmically, resulting in a close connection. The effect on relationships is highly positive when people communicate respectfully. For starters, the process is efficient, functioning like a well-oiled machine. Respectful people are not mired in confusion and misassumptions. They listen well, seek to understand, and choose their words carefully when speaking. Conversations can be brief yet beneficial, or lengthy with depth. Over time, the quality of relationships is broadened as individuals come to know one another.

One of the ways respect improves communication is in the regulation of power between individuals. As I discussed previously, power plays an important role in how people communicate. Power is an individual's right to think, feel, speak, and choose for oneself. When power is honored, individuals feel safe to express themselves. They will share their thoughts and feelings about a matter without fear of reprisal. Conversely, when power is not respected, the balance tips in favor of one person. This dynamic compromises safety and trust and inhibits the flow of communication. The relationship features one who is controlling and another who is passive-aggressive.

People seeking respectful relationships honor the power each one brings to the relationship. Neither person seeks to dominate the relationship; both honor the roles established. For example, in families, power can exist in a hierarchy where the status of parents outranks children. Parents model respect by encouraging their children to express themselves freely. They listen as the child or teenager says what they think or how they feel, or complain about what they don't like. This is a critical parenting skill that will affect the formation of a child's identity along the developmental path. Encouraging self-expression honors the inherent power within the child.

Having said this, a parent may decide not to agree with a child's requests or demands. Factors such as age, maturity, security, and family values often play a role in a parent's decision to decline a child's or teenager's request. A parent's decision to trump a child's choice with a No is not disrespecting the child's power. It is acting responsibly by doing what is ultimately best for the child under the circumstances.

We see this with Kevin and his daughter Stacy, where respect at this stage of their relationship has been one-sided. Having been an absentee dad, Kevin lost respect with Stacy. In her mind, she was confused by her father's recent actions. Kevin was becoming more involved as a parent and respectful to his wife and kids. When Stacy informed him that she would be home after curfew, Kevin told her he would not agree with her demand. He allowed her to express her opinion about curfew, but in the end he held to his parental veto. Stacy was angry with his decision and expressed her feelings toward him. Kevin did not stifle her in the moment, was tolerant of her anger, and clarified his decision in a respectful manner. He did not quell her emotions. In the end, Stacy would have to work through them, while she also wrestled with his decision to deny her request.

Respect not only improves communication; it is also facilitates conflict resolution. I talked about how families tend to stockpile their conflicts rather than resolve them. Bringing respect into relationships changes this negative pattern. Most people want closure to their disputes. Lingering problems drain energy, create distance, and leave people in a negative mood. Polarization ensues, pride dominates, and individuals become entrenched in their positions, often over matters that really don't matter.

When people agree to respect each other, they pay attention to two things: how they come across and what the other person is trying to communicate. If they are *reactive*—quick and impulsive—they risk becoming disrespectful. However, when they are *responsive*—slow and controlled—they will be respectful. Frustration and anger flare up in a conflict. By paying attention to how you are coming across in a conflict, you can tone it down and keep your emotions in check.

Paying attention to what the other person is trying to get across involves not only keeping your emotions in check, but also developing a listening ear. As I pointed out earlier, communication tools like understanding and validation reduce defensiveness and increase openness. In a conflict, you might respond by saying, *So what I hear you saying is….* Responding in this manner cues the person that what they say is important and you are trying to understand them. They are likely to lower their intensity and give a more calm and respectful response. Establishing a reciprocal pattern of dialog will help you address the matter safely and resolve the conflict with respect.

Deeper, More Trusting Relationships

Mutual respect takes relationships to deeper level. It's the law of reciprocity. If I show you respect and you respond in like manner, then we have established the basis for a trusting relationship. When trust exists between people, they rid themselves of protective barriers and open up to one another. With each exchange of openness, respect surfaces again, reinforcing trust and deepening the quality of the relationship. Of course, this doesn't happen overnight. Rather, it is established over time by a series of encounters exhibiting mutual respect—I show you respect, you show me respect.

This dynamic changed Kevin and Heidi's marriage. It came to a point when they decided that they would stop blaming all their problems on each other. Instead, they agreed to work on being respectful in every interaction. Respect was demonstrated in being courteous, polite, paying compliments, offering assistance, correcting faults, repairing conflicts, and seeking to accommodate each other when possible. It was awkward at first as they worked at changing this pattern. However, they soon saw the benefits of mutual respect. The frequency of arguments decreased, they got more accomplished, and they started to trust each other more. As they did, the couple started opening up more and their relationship deepened. Friendship paved the way for the return of intimacy to their marriage.

Establishing or rebuilding trust takes time. When working with couples where trust has been violated in some fashion, I give them a formula for rebuilding it. It looks like this:

$$\text{Formula for Trust}$$
$$\text{Trust} = \frac{\text{Behavior}}{\text{Time}}$$

The rebuilding of trust is contingent on the behavior of the other person being consistently congruent with their words over time. Specifically, their words and behavior have to match in a constant pattern day after day, week after week, month after month, year after year. The strength of trust is determined by the duration of time in which the trustworthy behavior is performed. In a relationship where infidelity violates trust, the involved spouse will have to convince the injured spouse by his or her behavior over time that they will honor the relationship by establishing and maintaining healthy boundaries with others. Injuries take time to heal and a wounded mate needs time to regain the trust that their partner will not cause any further harm.

When you are in a relationship that is equally benevolent, you have something special. You can feel safe with the person. Transparency is easier to exhibit because you trust the other individual is not going to cause you harm in words or actions. Rather, you experience unconditional acceptance, support, and compassion. The quality of the relationship is deep, satisfying, and secure. It doesn't mean you will never argue or go through rough patches. When things happen, you work through them faster and more efficiently because of the factors of respect and trust.

In my counseling practice, I observe this transformation not only in marriage relationships, but with parents and teens and among siblings. Beyond the family, respectful relationships can be formed at work, church, or other social environments. The key is reciprocity. In order for a relationship to go to a deeper level, both parties have to be willing to show respect. If you're doing it and the other person does not reciprocate, then you are unlikely to form a deep relationship. It may feel shallow, one-sided, and impersonal. Relationships of this sort typically do not have a long shelf life. On the contrary, individuals who establish a rhythm of respect and reciprocity form a wonderful relationship that is mutually rich and satisfying.

Where To Start Getting Respect Back

Getting respect back does not begin with your spouse, defiant teenager, or bossy sibling. Some think it would be easier if others would just treat them better. In family and marriage counseling, I sense the expectation clients have for me to get the "problem person" to behave. This approach does not have a high success rate.

Getting respect back begins with you getting your self-respect back. Here is where you need to start. Take a moment and answer the following questions honestly. Do you like being out of control? Are you proud of how you behave in a conflict? Have you justified your lack of self-control by blaming others? Do you make excuses for your bad habits by rationalizing how busy you are? When you look inside, do you like who you are? Do you silently beat yourself up with self-criticisms as you compare your performance with friends or family members?

If your responses to these questions indicates a struggle with self-respect, then I recommend you begin by taking better care of yourself. I know the tendency is to focus on others and the way they treat you, but if you don't have self-respect and set limits with people, they will likely not change their behavior. It may feel overwhelming to think about addressing your needs, particularly if you don't know where to start. Let me see if I could help you with some starters.

Our minds and bodies are synced; they operate in harmony. When one is not functioning well, the other is affected. Stress is one of those conditions that wreaks havoc on our minds and bodies. If you are mentally stressed, your brain releases stress hormones into the body, causing it to react in an abnormal way: upset stomach, ulcers, muscle ache, indigestion, headaches. Managing stress is therefore essential to overall health. Perhaps you can begin by thinking about what you are currently doing to manage stress and what you can begin doing or adding to your regimen.

There are several ways to manage stress, but I recommend that you choose strategies that address three areas: body, soul, and spirit. For the body, the obvious choices are diet and exercise. If you make a plan and execute it, you are already on a healthy path. For those who are just beginning, you may want to begin walking, stretching, and lowering your food intake. Establishing a routine in this area is key.

Several years ago, I joined a health club and started with a simple workout plan of light weightlifting. Later, I worked with a trainer who developed a more comprehensive plan that addressed my core. I also started playing pickup basketball games with some of the men at the club, playing once a week, advancing to twice a week, and occasionally three days. I've been doing this for well over a decade now and find it to be very beneficial in managing weight, releasing stress, and increasing overall fitness. There are certain types of exercise that work well to reduce physical and mental stress. Consider yoga or Pilates. It doesn't hurt to get an occasional massage, either.

For your soul, activities that treat your mind and emotions are beneficial. Relaxation and deep breathing exercises are excellent for reducing anxiety, slowing down your mind, and relaxing your body. Walks in nature, reading, journaling, doing crafts, gardening, art, or musical expression are just a few activities you can do to connect with yourself and fill your emotional tank. Investing time alone with yourself and doing things that resonate within is essential if you want to be a better version of yourself around people.

Do you know what you like to do that connects you with yourself? Take inventory of these things and perhaps add things you may want to try doing. You may not be able to do everything on your list, but at least you will have a few, if not more, things to choose. It is fascinating to watch my clients unpack their personal interests and put them into action. One of the guys is restoring an old car in his garage. A woman started taking yoga and has recently completed certification as a trainer. A young adult who came to me battling depression and anxiety during her high school years is now laying the groundwork for a book she wants to write for college students about managing mental illness while away at school. Where do you want to begin? Begin with something reasonable and doable. You'll build from there.

The third area of self-care is nurturing your spirit. The concept of spirit takes on different meanings. For those who have religious or spiritual roots, their belief in God may play a prominent role here. Others may have adopted their own view of spirituality that works for them. I have found in my counseling practice that people who believe in God tend to do better in resolving problems than those who do not. Research also indicates that spirituality plays a vital role in the mental health of individuals.

Do you have a spiritual orientation? How does it operate in your life today? Is it front and center? Is it on the back burner? I recommend you make it an active part of your daily life. Inviting God into your everyday life is a brilliant way to get your self-respect back. Who but an unconditional loving God can nurture your inner self with words of affirmation and hope?

I disclosed my spirituality earlier in the book. Having been raised in a Christian household, I learned early that God was someone I could always depend on to guide and help me find a path for my life. While there were times in my life I got off the path, I have found God to be an ever-present source of strength, comfort, and purpose. When I am stressed out or anxious about something, besides the body and soul routines, I go to God.

Two Bible verses have helped in particular when I am overwhelmed by the stressors of life. The first one says,[10] *"Cast all your anxiety on him, because he cares for you"*. The other one says,[11] *"Do not be anxious about anything, but in everything, by prayer and petition, with thanksgiving present your requests to God. And the peace of God which transcends all understanding will guard your hearts and your minds in Christ Jesus"*.

These verses fit perfectly with the exercise of letting out, letting go, and letting in. In letting out, I express all my anxieties and stresses to God. It is unfiltered, intense, and sometimes raw. In letting go, I give the things that trouble me or I cannot control to God. I cast my anxiety. Finally, in letting in, I do an exchange with God. I give him my anxiety and he gives me his peace to guard my heart and mind. My heart is my emotions. The peace of God helps me regulate my feelings so I don't stress out again. My mind is the thinking part of my brain that enables me to make good decisions in a stress-filled situation. Turning to God makes a huge difference in managing stress.

What is more important, knowing God cares for me not only reduces stress, but it reminds me that I have intrinsic value as one created in his image. Beyond what I think of myself, there is One who sees me as a unique being, crafted by his own hand and given the breath of life for a purpose. Knowing he respects the me he created encourages me to do likewise. Here, self-respect is powerfully woven into a relationship with a loving God.

Final Remarks

Well, I hope these three starters—body, soul, and spirit—will help you as you take the first step toward bringing respect back into your life. As you take that step, understand you are embarking on a major change in your personal life and interpersonal relationships. Be patient with yourself and others in this process. As I said previously, you will face

---

10   The Holy Bible - The Book of 1 Peter 5:8
11   The Holy Bible - The Book of Philippians 4:6-7

resistance from within and without, but if you are persistent, you will see respect come back in all phases of your life.

For those of you who find it really difficult to begin on your own because you are so heavily weighed down with burdens and suffer deep emotional pain, I recommend you seek professional support. Working with a professional counselor, psychologist, or therapist can help you deal with the emotional wounds that keep you stuck in place. I speak not only as one who provides the service, but as one who benefited from counseling when I was hurting and had somehow lost my self-respect. My hope for you is that you find a sojourner to walk alongside you in your journey.

In the opening chapter I stated that our culture has lost respect for respect. Perhaps at the conclusion of reading this book you have a new found respect for respect. May it begin with you respecting yourself more and making some decisions to bring this virtue back in a higher form. I also hope you will develop new ways, extracted from your reading, to show respect to others, beginning in your closest circle of relationships and moving out into your social world. As you bring respect back into your life and relationships your world will be much brighter.

Made in the USA
Lexington, KY
09 May 2014